Better Homes and Gardens®

Christmas from the Heart®

A Season of Giving

Better Homes and Gardens® Books
Des Moines, Iowa

Better Homes and Gardens® Books
An imprint of Meredith® Books

Christmas from the Heart: A Season of Giving
Editor: Carol Field Dahlstrom
Technical Editor: Susan M. Banker
Graphic Designer: Angie Hoogensen
Copy Chief: Catherine Hamrick
Copy and Production Editor: Terri Fredrickson
Contributing Technical Writer: Barbara Smith
Contributing Copy Editors: Jill Philby, Jennifer Speer Ramundt
Contributing Proofreader: Colleen Johnson
Technical Illustrator: Chris Neubauer Graphics, Inc.
Electronic Production Coordinator: Paula Forest
Editorial and Design Assistants: Judy Bailey, Kaye Chabot, Treesa Landry, Karen Schirm
Production Director: Douglas M. Johnston
Production Manager: Pam Kvitne
Assistant Prepress Manager: Marjorie J. Schenkelberg

Meredith® Books
Editor in Chief: James D. Blume
Design Director: Matt Strelecki
Managing Editor: Gregory H. Kayko

Director, Sales & Marketing, Retail: Michael A. Peterson
Director, Sales & Marketing, Special Markets: Rita McMullen
Director, Sales & Marketing, Home & Garden Center Channel: Ray Wolf
Director, Operations: George A. Susral

Vice President, General Manager: Jamie L. Martin

Better Homes and Gardens® **Magazine**
Editor in Chief: Jean LemMon

Meredith Publishing Group
President, Publishing Group: Christopher M. Little
Vice President, Consumer Marketing & Development: Hal Oringer

Meredith Corporation
Chairman and Chief Executive Officer: William T. Kerr

Chairman of the Executive Committee: E. T. Meredith III

Cover Photograph: Hopkins Associates

All of us at Better Homes and Gardens® Books are dedicated to providing you with information and ideas to create beautiful and useful projects. We welcome your comments and suggestions. Write to us at: Better Homes and Gardens® Books, Crafts Editorial Department, 1716 Locust Street, Des Moines, IA 50309-3023.

ISBN: 0-696-20724-9
ISSN: 1081-4698

Our seal assures you that every recipe in *Christmas from the Heart: A Season of Giving* has been tested in the Better Homes and Gardens® Test Kitchen. This means that each recipe is practical and reliable, and meets our high standards of taste appeal. We guarantee your satisfaction with this book for as long as you own it.

®   If you would like to order additional copies of this book, call 800/439-7159.

a SEASON of giving

Many years ago the greatest gift of all was given—the Christ Child. The celebration of that event we call Christmas fills our hearts with the spirit of giving year after year. Many times gifts appear as sweetly wrapped goodies tucked into stockings or nestled under the Christmas tree. Sometimes they are handmade heirlooms or delicious treats made in the kitchen. Other times a gift of kindness or understanding is all we need, or a gift of experience is what we share. However you choose to celebrate the first gift, we hope this book will inspire you to make this the most memorable of holidays and the most glorious Season of Giving.

CONTENTS

Comfort and Joy

Let Heaven and Nature Sing

Simple Gifts

Make a Joyful Noise

A Season of Giving

A Star in the East

Happy Holiday Celebrations

Symbols of the Season

Christmas Housewarming

comfort & JOY

Tidings of comfort and joy—what could be
a finer gift! From mittens to Santas, from
snowmen to sweaters, we'll help you create
loving gifts to give, jolly friends to cherish,
and delightful comforts for your home.

candy cane
SCARF SET

She'll stay warm and toasty dressed in her candy cane scarf, mittens, and hat knit from soft red and eggshell-color yarns. The hat has a jolly bell tassel and the scarf has fancy fringe. Instructions are on page 16.

Design: Ann E. Smith for Spinrite

joyful
GIFT BAG
santa

Santa is always filled with joy, but our Santa, filled with sweet candies, is extra special. His body is a bag made to hold holiday goodies. A red and gold drawstring keeps the candy safe inside. Full-size patterns and instructions begin on page 17.

Design: Phyllis Dunstan

gingerbread man
GOODY JAR & MUGS

Come in from the cold and feel the warmth of a delightful cup of hot chocolate served in a decorated gingerbread man mug. We've filled our matching cookie jar with popcorn balls, but any goody will do the trick. A painted gingerbread man napkin rests underneath our holiday treats. Instructions begin on page 20.

Design: Susan Banker

dainty
WELCOME
towel

Making your guests feel comfortable at the holiday season is a real gift. What better way to make them feel at home than to display welcome wishes on a lovely guest towel. Embroidered with floss and ribbons, this towel is quick to stitch. The instructions and chart are on page 21.

Design: Phyllis Dobbs

happy snowman
FAMILY

Pleased to be propped upon the mantel, or any spot in the house, our snowman family will bring smiles from your wintertime guests. Made from gourds, fabric, a bit of clay, and paint, each snow person has a playful personality. Step-by-step instructions for the bunch are on pages 22–23.

Design: Alice Wetzel

cuddly
SNOWMEN
sweater

It may be cold outside, but inside it's time for tea with special friends. Our tea server is dressed for the day in a comfy sweater knit with acrylic yarn. Instructions and pattern are on pages 24–25.

Design: Ann E. Smith for Reynolds

snuggly
VELVET MITTENS

Keep those fingers snug and warm with our printed velvet mittens. The design is made using rubber stamps, and the effect is truly unique. The mittens are trimmed with fake fur for an elegant touch. The instructions and pattern are on pages 25–26.

Design: Margaret Sindelar

Candy Cane Scarf Set

As shown on page 8.

SIZE
For children ages 5–10 years

SKILL LEVEL
For the intermediate knitter

MATERIALS FOR THE SET
Lily's Sugar 'n Cream yarn: four skeins red (95) and three skeins eggshell (05)
Sizes 5 and 7 straight knitting needles or size to obtain gauge below
Size 5 double-pointed knitting needles (dpn)
Yarn needle; one small stitch holder
Cable needle (cn)

GAUGE
In stockinette stitch (st st) with larger needles, 17 sts and 25 rows = 4 inches.

ABBREVIATIONS
See page 160.

CABLE PATTERN
Row 1 (RS): P 2; place the next 3 sts onto cn and hold at back of work, k 3 sts, k 3 sts from cn; slip the next 3 sts onto cn and hold at front of work, k 3 sts, k 3 sts from cn; p 2.
Row 2: K 2, p 12, k 2.
Row 3: P 2, k 12, p 2.
Rows 4–9: Rep rows 2–3.
Row 10: Rep Row 2.

INSTRUCTIONS
Mittens
Right Hand: With smaller straight needles and red, cast on 31 sts.

For ribbing, Row 1 (RS): K 1, * p 1, k 1; rep from * across. Row 2: P 1, * k 1, p 1; rep from * across. Rep rows 1–2 to 2½ inches from beginning, ending with Row 2 and inc 4 sts evenly spaced on the last row = 35 sts.

Change to the larger straight needles. Row 1 (RS): K 1, p 2, k 12, p 2, k 18. Row 2: P 1, k 2, p 12, k 2, p 18.

Change to white; k 1, work Row 1 of Cable Pat on next 16 sts, k 18.

Row 2: P 18, Cable Pat on 16 sts, p 1.

Rows 3–4: Work in est pat.

Row 5: K 1, Cable Pat on 16 sts, (slip horizontal running thread between last st and next st onto left needle, k in back lp of this new st = M 1 made), k 2, M 1, k to end.

Row 6: P 20, Cable Pat on 16 sts, p 1.

Row 7: K 1, Cable 16, M 1, k 4, M 1, k to end.

Row 8: P 22, Cable 16, p 1.

Row 9: K 1, Cable 16, M 1, k 6, M 1, k to end.

Row 10: P 24, Cable 16, p 1.

Change to red; k 1, work Row 1 of Cable Pat on next 16 sts, place next 8 sts onto a small holder, k 16. Cont on these 33 sts in cable and striped pat for one red and one white stripe. With red, work as est for 6 rows.

For shaping, Row 1: * K2tog, k 1; rep from * across. Row 2: P 22. Row 3: * K 1, k2tog across, ending k 1. Row 4: P 15.

For top, leaving a long tail for sewing, cut yarn. Thread tail into yarn needle and back through rem 15 sts; pull up to tightly close opening. Using matching yarn colors, join sides.

To complete thumb, arrange sts from holder onto 3 dpn. Join white and k 8; pick up and k 3 sts along top edge. K around and around for 7 rnds. (K2tog, k 1) around, ending k2tog = 7 sts. K 1 rnd. K 1, (k2tog) around = 4 sts. Finish as for the mitten top.

Left Hand: Work as for the Right Hand through completion of ribbing. Change to larger straight needles. Row 1 (RS): K 18, p 2, k 12, p 2, k 1. Reversing Cable Pat and thumb, work as for the Right Hand.

Hat
With larger straight needles and red, cast on 86 sts.

Row 1 (WS): P 1, (k 1, p 1) across next 34 sts, k 2, p 12, k 2, (p 1, k 1) across the next 34 sts, p 1.

Row 2: K 1, (p 1, k 1) across next 34 sts, Row 1 of Cable Pat on 16 sts, (k 1, p 1) on 34 sts, k 1.

Row 3: Rep Row 1.

Row 4: K 35, Row 3 of Cable Pat on 16 sts, k 35.

Row 5: P 35, Row 4 of Cable Pat on 16 sts, p 35.

Cont est pat through completion of Cable Pat, Row 10; cut red and join white yarn. Working center 16 sts in Cable Pat and 35 sts along edge side in st st work one white stripe and one red stripe. Change to white and work 6 rows of Cable Pat.

For crown shaping, with white (k2tog, k 1) across, ending k2tog. P 57. K 1, (k2tog) across. P 29. Change to red, k 1, (k2tog) across. P 15. K 1, (k2tog) across. P 8. Leaving a sewing tail, cut yarn. Thread tail through rem sts and pull tightly to close top. Using matching yarn colors, sew back seam.

For tassel (make two), cut 17 red strands each measuring 14 inches. Holding strands together, tie a separate strand of red tightly around center. Fold strands in half and tie another red strand tightly ½-inch from top. Attach to top of hat.

Scarf
With larger straight needles and red, cast on 60 sts. P 22, k 2, p 12, k 2, p 22. Keeping 22 sts along edge, edge in st st and beginning with Row 1 of Cable Pat on center 16 sts, work 10 rows red and 10 rows white for 23 stripes. Bind off all sts. Using matching yarn colors, sew back seam.

For fringe, cut 7 strands of red each measuring about 16 inches. Holding strands together, fold in half to form a loop. Pull loop through center of cable; draw ends through loop and pull up to form a knot. Alternating colors, add four more bundles of fringe along side of center bundle of fringe. Repeat for opposite edge.

Joyful Gift Bag Santa

As shown on page 9, finished Santa is 26 inches long.

MATERIALS

Yardages are for 45-inch-wide fabrics
Tracing paper
⅓ yard of red wide-wale corduroy
¼ yard of black polished cotton fabric
¼ yard of ecru cotton fabric
4x4-inch piece of muslin
**4x4-inch piece of paper-backed
    iron-on adhesive**
8x14-inch piece of white satin
**10x20-inch piece of gold
    metallic netting**
**Three 1x5-inch strips of white
    short-nap fake fur**
Fabric marking pen
Thread to match fabrics
**⅔ yard of red 1-inch-wide double-fold
    bias tape**
Pins
Polyester fiberfill
Ten ⅜-inch-diameter gold jingle bells
Black ultra-fine tip permanent marker
2 yards of gold and red cording
Two 5mm black beads; crafts glue
1½-inch-diameter white pom-pom
Cosmetic powder blush

Open

**GIFT BAG SANTA
    BOOT**

INSTRUCTIONS

Trace patterns, *below* and *pages 18–19*, onto paper and cut out. Fold corduroy, black polished cotton, and ecru cotton fabrics in half with right sides facing. Use fabric marker to draw around leg and arm patterns twice and hat pattern once on corduroy. Draw around boot pattern twice on black cotton and hand pattern twice onto ecru cotton. *Do not* cut out pieces.

For head, fuse iron-on adhesive square to muslin square following manufacturer's instructions. Draw around face pattern on muslin; cut out. Cut satin into two 8×7-inch pieces. Remove paper backing from face. Referring to head pattern, position face on right side of one satin piece; fuse in place. Machine-stitch around face using narrow zigzag stitches and black thread. Turn piece over and position head pattern on back, aligning stitched face outline with face outline on head pattern. Draw around head pattern. Position satin piece with face atop the other, right sides together.

For all pieces, sew on drawn lines on doubled fabrics, leaving openings as marked on patterns. Cut out pieces ¼ inch beyond stitching; clip curves. Turn right side out and set aside.

Fold gold netting in half to measure 10×10 inches with fold at bottom. Center legs between layers, with top edges of legs against netting's folded edge. Sew across folded edge of netting ¼ inch away from fold to secure leg tops.

Measure 1¼ inches down from top edges of folded netting and insert arm on each side, matching top edges of arms with side raw edges of netting.

Sew ¼-inch seam down each netting side, leaving top 1¼ inches on each side unstitched.

Turn netting bag right side out. Cut two strips of bias tape to measure length of top edge of bag plus ½ inch. Turn under each end of tape ¼ inch; stitch to netting's raw edge. Fold each strip over top edge of bag; stitch.

Stuff mittens to within ½ inch of opening. Stuff arms; sew openings closed. Slip a mitten over end of each arm and whipstitch wrist edges of mittens to arms. Trim fur strip for each wrist to fit; glue around mitten.

Stuff boots; stitch across openings to close. Stuff each leg to within ½ inch of opening. Turn under ¼ inch along raw edges. Using a doubled thread and running stitches, run a gathering thread along each fold. Insert boot tops into bottom of legs and pull gathering threads to close legs around boots. Adjust gathers and tack leg edges to boots. Sew five bells around gathered bottom edge of each pant leg.

Cut cord into two equal lengths for drawstring. Beginning at one side of bag, thread one cord all the way around through both bag top casings and out again at starting point. Knot ends together. Repeat with remaining cord, beginning on opposite side.

Stuff head; sew opening closed. Using black thread, sew black beads in place for eyes. Pull thread tight between eyes to define bridge of nose. Using same thread, straight-stitch eyebrows. Enter and exit through head top to hide thread ends. Use black marker to add detail to inner eyes and nostrils as desired.

Stuff hat to within ¾ inch of opening. Turn under ¼ inch along raw edge; blindstitch hat to head. Trim remaining fur strip to fit along bottom front edge of hat; glue. Sew pom-pom to hat tip.

Center head on bag's front casing. Whipstitch casing to head back, sewing only through top and bottom edges of casing so cord does not get caught in stitches.

Add blush to cheeks, nostrils, and tip of nose to complete face.

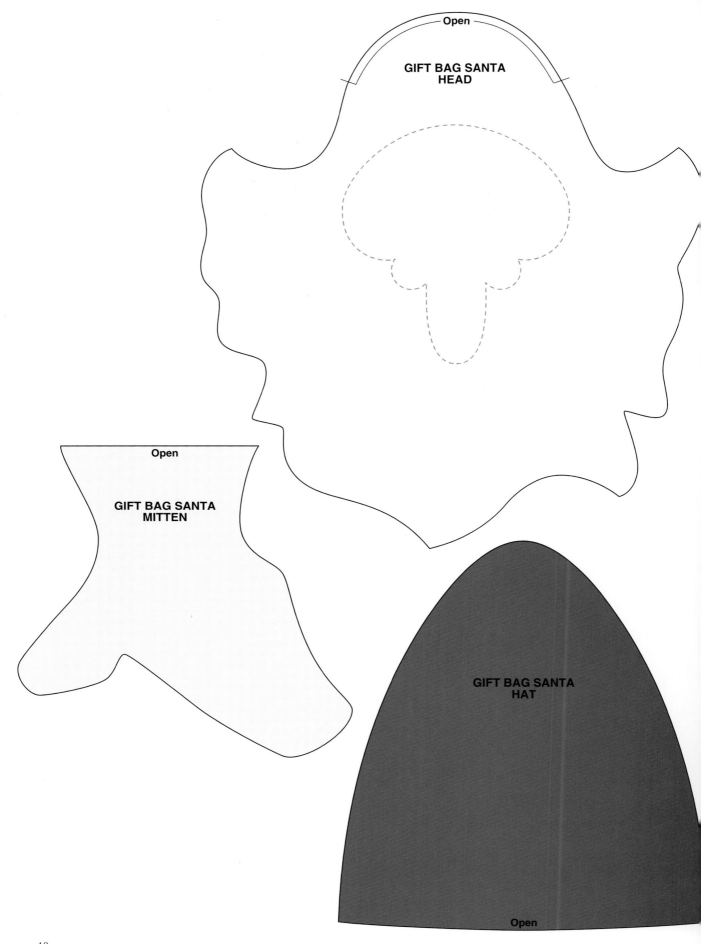

Open

GIFT BAG SANTA
HEAD

Open

GIFT BAG SANTA
MITTEN

GIFT BAG SANTA
HAT

Open

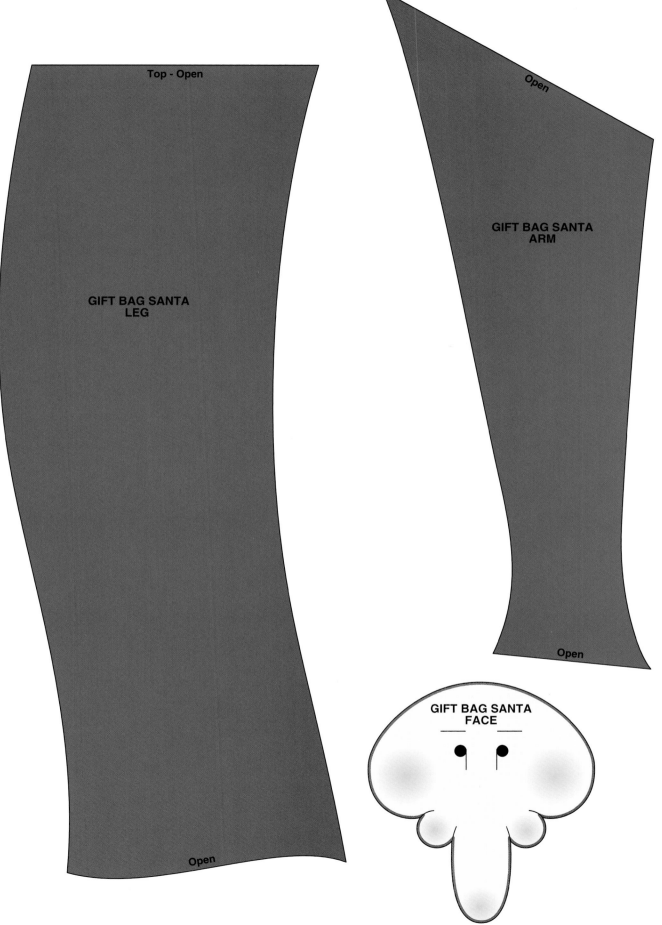

Top - Open

GIFT BAG SANTA
LEG

Open

Open

GIFT BAG SANTA
ARM

Open

GIFT BAG SANTA
FACE

Gingerbread Man Goody Jar & Mugs

As shown on page 10.

MATERIALS

Clear glass cookie jar and mugs
Liquitex Glossies high gloss acrylic
    enamel paints for glass: golden
    brown, green, white, red, and
    metallic gold
½-inch-wide flat paintbrush
Small round paintbrush
Tracing paper
Tape

INSTRUCTIONS

Wash and dry cookie jar and mugs thoroughly. Avoid touching the surfaces to be painted.

For cookie jar, use flat brush and red paint to paint two rows of checkerboard pattern around the curved bottom edge of jar. Allow paint to dry. Using green paint, complete checkerboard pattern; allow to dry.

Trace large gingerbread man goody jar pattern, *right,* onto tracing paper; cut out. Tape pattern, slightly angled, to inside of cookie jar 1 inch from bottom. Using flat brush, golden brown paint, and pattern as a guide, paint gingerbread man. Repeat, painting gingerbread men at different angles around outside of jar. Allow paint to dry.

Paint evergreen wisps above the gingerbread men using flat brush, green paint, and the photograph, *page 10,* as a guide. When green paint is dry, brush white paint lightly over green for a snowy effect.

Outline each gingerbread man using round brush and white paint using a zigzag motion. Add white mouth and eyes to each. Paint small round noses and buttons red. Highlight buttons with white.

Dip eraser end of pencil in desired color paint and press onto glass repeatedly to make garland between greens as shown in photograph.

GINGERBREAD MAN GOODY JAR

GINGERBREAD MAN NAPKIN

GINGERBREAD MAN MUG

Paint gold swirls at random between gingerbread men using round brush.

Allow the paint to dry 24 hours. Bake the cookie jar in oven at 325 degrees for 35 minutes. Keep area well ventilated. After baking time, turn oven off and allow jar to cool in oven. When completely cool, paint is permanent.

For each mug, paint only one row of green and red checkerboard border, following method for cookie jar, *left.* Trace gingerbread man mug pattern onto tracing paper; cut out. Tape pattern at an angle to inside of mug ½ inch from bottom. Paint as for cookie jar.

Paint a second gingerbread man on the opposite side of the mug. Paint the details on gingerbread men and add swirls as for the cookie jar.

Bake mug, following directions given for cookie jar.

Gingerbread Man Napkin
As shown on page 10.

MATERIALS
Purchased red napkin
Transfer paper; transfer pen
Fabric paints: brown and white
½-inch flat paintbrush
Small round paintbrush
12 inches of ⅛-inch-wide green satin ribbon
Needle; green sewing thread

INSTRUCTIONS
Wash, dry, and iron napkin.

Trace gingerbread man napkin pattern, *page 20*, onto transfer paper using transfer pen. Following manufacturer's instructions, transfer gingerbread man outline to one corner of napkin and again to each side of the first.

Paint gingerbread men brown; allow to dry. Outline each gingerbread man in white, using a zigzag motion. Paint mouth and dot eyes and buttons white; allow to dry completely.

Cut ribbon into three 4-inch-long pieces; tie each in bow. Tack a bow to the neck of each gingerbread man.

Dainty Welcome Towel
As shown on page 11.

MATERIALS
FABRIC
White fingertip towel with 14-count Aida insert
THREADS
Bucilla embroidery ribbon in the colors listed in key, below
Cotton embroidery floss in colors listed in key, below

DAINTY WELCOME TOWEL

Green sewing thread
Red sewing thread
SUPPLIES
Tapestry, chenille, and beading needles
Embroidery hoop
Seed beads in colors listed in key

INSTRUCTIONS
Find center of chart and center of Aida insert; begin stitching there.

Use three plies of embroidery floss to work all stitches.

Work ribbon embroidery stitches using chenille needle. Attach beads using coordinating thread.

Japanese Leaf Stitch

Lazy Daisy Stitch

Loop Stitch

Stem Stitch

DAINTY WELCOME TOWEL

Anchor	DMC	
212	☒	561 Dark seafoam

JAPANESE LEAF STITCH
- 539 Red Bucilla 4mm embroidery ribbon
- 628 Forest green Bucilla 4mm embroidery ribbon

LAZY DAISY STITCH
- 539 Red Bucilla 4mm embroidery ribbon
- 628 Forest green Bucilla 4mm embroidery ribbon

LOOP STITCH
- 503 Pale honey yellow Bucilla 7mm embroidery ribbon

STEM STITCH
- 628 Forest green Bucilla 4mm embroidery ribbon

MILL HILL BEADS
- 02013 Red red seed bead
- 00332 Emerald seed bead

Stitch count: 33 high x 56 wide
Finished design sizes:
14-count fabric – 2⅜ x 4 inches
16-count fabric – 2⅛ x 3½ inches
18-count fabric – 1⅞ x 3⅛ inches

Snowman Family

As shown on pages 12–13, snowmen range from 9½ to 12 inches tall.

MATERIALS FOR ONE SNOWMAN
Hardened light-brown hollow dried gourd in snowman shape
Sharp non-serrated knife
8x30-inch strip of burlap
Mod Podge decoupage sealer; bowl
Cotton sock or doll's black hat to fit head; small decorative bird
White sewing thread; needle
Acrylic paints: deep blue, white, black, orange, and desired colors for scarf and cap
Small sponge
Artists' and 1- and 2-inch paintbrushes
Crayola Model Magic clay
Gel Superglue; black paint pen
Acrylic satin spray varnish; buttons
Embroidery floss; large jingle bell

INSTRUCTIONS
Clean gourd as shown in Step 1, *below,* and dry surface.

Cut burlap for scarf (see Step 2, *below).* Remove several threads along edges to make ½-inch-long fringe. Wet scarf and wring out excess water. Dip scarf into the Mod Podge as shown in Step 3, *below.* Tie scarf around snowman's neck.

To make stocking cap, cut stocking as shown in Step 4, *below.*

1

Soak gourd in warm soapy water several hours. Using a knife held at an angle, scrape off outer layer of skin. Use a kitchen scrubber to remove any remaining skin.

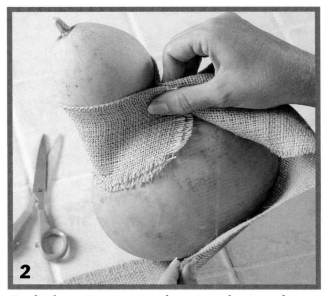

2

Cut burlap strip to measure three times the circumference of neck area on gourd. Fold strip in half lengthwise. Tie around neck and trim to desired length; remove scarf.

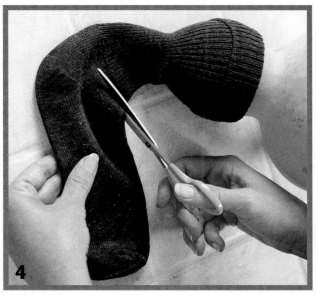

3

Pour Mod Podge into bowl. Dip scarf into bowl, working Mod Podge thoroughly into fabric. Let dry. Tie scarf around snowman, arranging fabric as desired.

4

Cuff sock about 1 inch and pull down over gourd head. Determine desired length, and cut off excess. Remove sock, turn inside out, and sew cut end closed.

Soak cap in water, wring out excess, and work Mod Podge into cap as for scarf. Position cap on head; cuff bottom edge and shape as desired.

Allow scarf and cap to dry several hours or overnight until hard.

Paint snowman as shown in Steps 5–7, *below*. Paint cap and scarf with desired pattern, using paint thinned to consistency of cream. Apply paint lightly to allow fabric texture to show. Follow direction of ribbing or threads of fabric as a guide for pattern, referring to photograph, *pages 12–13*, for ideas.

Make eyes and nose as shown in Step 8, *below*. When dry, highlight eyes with white; wipe nose with blue paint, removing excess for an antiqued effect. Glue eyes and nose in place. Using paint pen, draw large curved mouth beneath nose. Allow all glue and paint to dry.

Spray the entire snowman with varnish and allow it to dry. If desired, glue a jingle bell to the end of the stocking cap.

For snowman with black hat, glue hat to head at angle. Glue bird to top of hat.

Layer colorful buttons by sewing one atop the other using scraps of embroidery floss, if desired. Glue buttons down center front of snowman.

5

Put the hat on the snowman; let dry. Paint the entire snowman blue, working paint well into the stiffened fabric of scarf and cap. Allow paint to dry thoroughly.

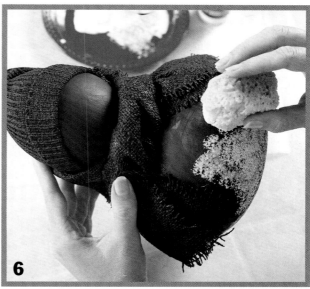

6

Thin white paint until transparent. Using sponge, apply layers of thinned paint to gourd surface. Use caution near edges of scarf and cap, allowing blue to remain.

7

To finish, use water to thin white paint and paint open areas of the body. Thin colored paints and paint cap and scarf with desired pattern.

8

Mold clay into two ½-inch-diameter round or oval eyes and one 1⅛-inch-long nose and allow to dry until hard. Paint eyes black and nose orange; allow to dry.

Snowmen Sweater

As shown on page 14, sweater is a child's size 4.

As shown on page 14,

SIZES
Instructions given are for child's size 4; changes for sizes 6, 8, and 10 follow in parentheses. Finished chest size = 27(30½, 34, 37½) inches.

SKILL LEVEL
For the experienced knitter

MATERIALS
Unger Utopia, a worsted weight acrylic yarn (100-gram or 240-yard skein): two(three, three, three) skeins of red (236); one(one, one, two) skeins of black (104); and for all sizes, one skein *each* of oatmeal (35), white (200), and green (299)
Size 5 and 7 straight knitting needles or size to obtain gauge below
Size 5 circular needle in 16-inch-length
Yarn needle; 11 bobbins

GAUGE
In Basketweave Pattern, 27 sts = 6 inches and 7 rows = 1 inch.
In Stockinette Stitch and color patterns, 14 sts = 3 inches and 7 rows = 1 inch.

ABBREVIATIONS
See page 160.

PATTERN STITCH
BASKETWEAVE PATTERN
Row 1 (WS): P 1 st for selvage edge, * k 5 sts, p 3 sts; rep from * across, ending k 5 sts, p 1 st for selvage edge.
Row 2: K 1, * p 5, k 3; rep from * across, ending p 5, k 1.
Row 3: Rep Row 1.
Row 4: Knit across.
Row 5: P 1, k 1, * p 3, k 5; rep from * across, ending p 3, k 1, p 1.
Row 6: K 1, p 1, * k 3, p 5; rep from * across, ending k 3, p 1, k 1.
Row 7: Rep Row 5.
Row 8: Knit across.
Rep rows 1–8 for Basketweave Pat.

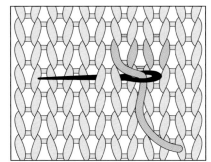

Duplicate Stitch

INSTRUCTIONS
Notes: Pine trees and snowmen hats are added in duplicate stitch after knitting is completed. Bobbins are recommended for knitting the snowmen in st st. When changing color, bring new color from under previous color for a twist to prevent holes.
Back: With smaller needles and black, cast on 63(71, 79, 87) sts.

For ribbing, Row 1 (RS): K 1, * p 1, k 1; rep from * across.

Row 2: P 1, * k 1, p 1; rep from * across.

Rep Rows 1–2 to 2 inches from beg, ending with a RS row. Change to larger needles.

For Pine Tree Border: P 1 row black. Change to oatmeal and work 6 rows st st. Change to black and k 1 row.

For Basketweave Pat: Change to red and p 1 row, k 1 row. Rep Rows 1–8 of Basketweave Pat for 3(4, 5, 6) times.

Work Pine Tree Border as est.

For Snowmen: P 1 row oatmeal. Working in st st, beg Snowmen Chart at #4(#2, #3, #1) and work to C; rep A–C once for all sizes; for size 8 and 10, work A–B once; for all sizes, end chart by working from D to #5(#7, #6, #8) = 4(4, 5, 5) snowmen. Complete chart.

Work Pine Tree Border as est.

Change to red. P 1 row, k 1 row. Work Basketweave Rows 1–8 for 3 times. Bind off all sts.

Front: Work as for Back through completion of third Pine Tree Border. Change to red. P 1 row, k 1 row. Work Basketweave rows 1–7. Row 8: K 22(25, 28, 31) sts; join a new strand of red and bind off the center 19(21, 23, 25) sts;

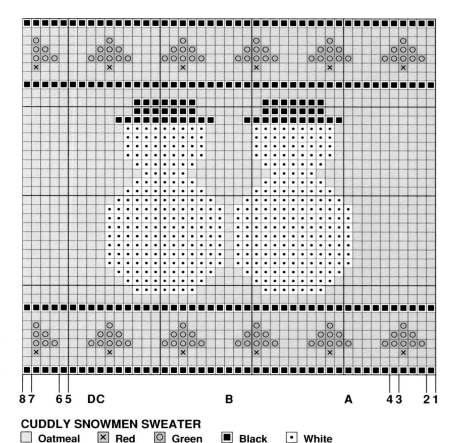

8 7   6 5   D C   B   A   4 3   2 1

CUDDLY SNOWMEN SWEATER
☐ Oatmeal   ☒ Red   ⊙ Green   ■ Black   ⊡ White

k to end of row. Keeping to est pat, working sides at the same time and with separate strands, dec 1 st at each neck edge every other row 3 times = 19(22, 25, 28) sts rem for each shoulder. Work even to same length as Back. Bind off all sts.

For sleeves (make two): With smaller needles and black, cast on 31(33, 35, 37) sts. Work Ribbing as for Back to 3 inches from beg, ending with a WS row. Rib across next RS row, inc 16(14, 12, 10) sts evenly spaced = 47 sts. Change to larger needles and work Pine Tree Border. Change to red; p 1 row, k 1 row. Work Rows 1–3 of Basketweave. On Row 4, k across and inc 1 st in second st from each edge = 49 sts. Including new sts into Basketweave pat, inc as est every sixth row for 4(6, 8, 10) times more = 57(61, 65, 69) sts. Cont est pat until sleeve measures 13½(15, 15½, 16) inches from beg, ending with Row 3 or Row 7. Bind off all sts knitwise.

Finishing: Join shoulder seams. Place markers 6¾(7, 7½, 8) inches from shoulder seam and along each edge. Set in sleeves bet markers.

Embroider pine trees with duplicate st in each oatmeal area following Cuddly Snowmen Sweater chart, *left.*

Using matching colors, join sleeve and side seams.

Neckband: With the RS facing, using circular needle and red, beg at a shoulder seam and pick up and k 70(74, 78, 82) sts evenly spaced around. Place a marker to indicate beg of rnd. Change to black and k 1 rnd. With black, work k 1, p 1 ribbing around for 13 rnds. Bind off loosely in ribbing. Fold band to inside and whipstitch in place. Weave in loose ends.

Velvet Mittens

As shown on page 15, mittens fit medium-size adult hand.

MATERIALS FOR ONE PAIR
Iron; ½ yard of 45-inch-wide velvet (silk, rayon, or acetate-rayon in desired color, *not* nylon, polyester, or washable velvet)
Heat embossing stamp of choice
Tracing paper
½ yard of polar fleece in desired color
½ yard of ¼-inch-wide elastic
4x18-inch strip of black or white fake fur; thread to match velvet
10–16 gold star buttons (optional)

INSTRUCTIONS

Turn iron to wool or cotton setting *without* steam. To emboss velvet, mist right side of fabric with water. Place fabric stamp right side up on hard surface. With right side of fabric positioned over stamp, press with steady iron for 20 seconds; remove.

Enlarge and trace pattern, *page 26,* onto tracing paper. Pattern may be made slightly smaller or larger around curved edges to fit hand.

Cut two mitten shapes from velvet, reverse pattern, and cut two more. Repeat to cut lining pieces from fleece. Determine velvet and fleece lining palm pieces for each mitten; trim ¼ inch from outside curved edge of palm pieces.

For each mitten, sew velvet pieces together for 6 inches along side seam opposite thumb, beginning at wrist edge. Use ¼-inch seam allowance. Open the piece out flat and on wrong side, mark a horizontal line across palm piece only, 3½ inches from wrist edge. Stretch elastic across this line and zigzag-stitch in place; trim excess elastic. Fold pieces back together with right sides facing. Sew remainder of outside seam, easing top mitten piece to palm piece. Double stitch at thumb as shown on the pattern.

Repeat for polar piece lining. Clip seams where thumb joins hand section. Turn velvet outer mittens right side out. Slip lining into each mitten, matching side seams. Baste around wrist edges.

Cut fur strip to measure 2½ inches longer than wrist edge. Trim short ends of fur at an angle as shown on diagram, *left.* Sew ends of each strip together, making center back seam. With right side of fur facing right side of lining, match short edge of fur to wrist; stitch. Turn cuffs to right side.

Turn bottom edge of cuffs under ¼ inch; handstitch to hem. If desired, sew buttons to mitten fronts.

SNUGGLY VELVET MITTENS
Fur Strip Trimming Diagram

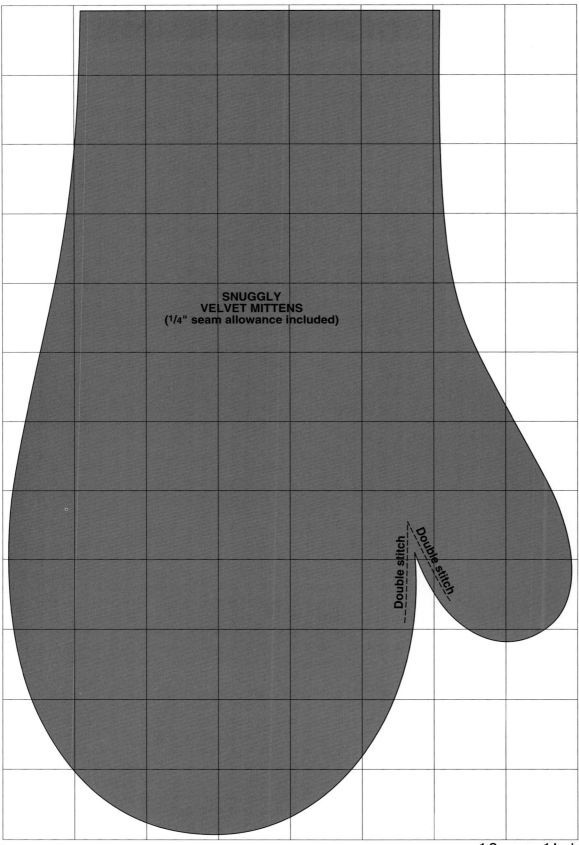

**SNUGGLY
VELVET MITTENS
(¹/₄" seam allowance included)**

Double stitch

Double stitch

1 Square = 1 Inch

let heaven & NATURE sing

Giving back to nature, even in a small way, is a wonderful gesture to convey all year long. At Christmastime, your love of nature can be displayed by feeding the birds on an evergreen tree, by decorating with nature's own lovely motifs, or by creating works of art with scenes from the outdoors. Whatever way you choose to give back to nature, we know you'll be pleasing all of your outdoor friends.

STARRY
birdhouses

Made in three sizes to make all your feathered friends happy, our birdhouses are painted in holiday colors to celebrate the season. Two of our birdhouses feature a star shape for little ones to pass through. Instructions are on page 36.

Design: Gaylen Chesnut

for the birds
CHRISTMAS
tree

Naturally the birds will love a holiday tree created just for them. Filled with all kinds of goodies, we've wrapped our tree with grapevines and added a sunflower topper. For a closer look at the ornaments, see the next page.

Design: Donna Chesnut and Carol Dahlstrom

toast the birds
TRIMS

Toast trims, birdseed cradles made from lemons and limes, and a garland strung with cherries, bread, and sunflower seeds all combine to make a tree fit for the birds. Let the children help pick the cookie-cutter shapes, then have fun serving lunch to the birds outdoors. Instructions for making the toast trims are on page 37.

Design: Donna Chesnut and Carol Dahlstrom

into the woods
FELT ORNAMENTS

Our animals from the woods are cut from felt and positioned on a homespun fabric, creating rustic yet festive ornaments for any room. Trimmed with zigzagged felt, the pieces are sure to become holiday favorites. Instructions are on pages 37–38.

Design: Studio B

log cabin
STOCKING

Designed for friends of the outdoors, our felt stocking is a collection of favorite nature motifs. The rich colors and textures of the outdoors blend to create a natural holiday look. Complete instructions and patterns are on pages 38–40.

Design: Studio B

nature's own
FRUIT WREATH

The bold and natural colors of nature inspired this holiday fruit wreath. Easy to create yet impressive to look at, we have given you step-by-step instructions for making the wreath. Instructions are on page 41.

Design: Leonhard's Garden Center, Beverly, MA

nature lover's
CROSS-STITCH

Elegantly displaying the love of nature, this cross-stitch piece is sure to be displayed all year long. The intricate work is stitched on 28-count light blue Jobelan and showcases some lovely specialty stitches. Chart and instructions are on pages 42–44.

Design: Barbara Sestok

Starry Birdhouses

As shown on pages 28–29, the saltbox birdhouse is 7¾×7¾×7½ inches, two-story birdhouse is 12½×7×7½ inches, and small birdhouse is 4¾×5×5 inches.

MATERIALS
FOR SALTBOX BIRDHOUSE
4 feet of ½×8-inch pine
½-inch-long piece of ⅜-inch dowel
For two-story birdhouse
6 feet of ½×8-inch pine
FOR SMALL PLYWOOD BIRDHOUSE
12×12-inch piece of ¼-inch plywood
FOR ALL BIRDHOUSES
Tracing paper; carbon paper; jigsaw
Drill; drill bits; wood glue; hammer
1-inch brad nails; latex paint in desired colors; paintbrush; sandpaper

INSTRUCTIONS
For saltbox birdhouse
Cut one 7½×6-inch bottom piece, one 6×4¾-inch side piece, one 6×2-inch side piece, one 5×7-inch roof piece, one 7×6-inch roof piece, and two 6⅝×6-inch front/back pieces from pine.

Enlarge and trace roofline and star from pattern, *right,* onto tracing paper. Transfer roof line to top of front and back pieces using carbon paper between pattern and wood. Transfer star to front piece. Using jigsaw, cut roof angles. Drill a ¾-inch hole in center of traced star; cut star points with jigsaw. Drill ⅜-inch hole 1 inch below star to hold perch.

Glue a side piece to the front piece; secure with brads. Glue the second side piece to the front; secure with brads. Attach back piece to sides in same manner. Apply a bead of glue along bottom edges of assembly; attach bottom piece with back edges flush. Secure with brads. Attach larger roof piece, taking care to align top edge with point on front and back. Glue and nail smaller roof piece, with top edge overlapping larger roof piece. Glue dowel into hole for perch.

Apply one coat of paint to birdhouse; allow to dry. Sand lightly for a worn appearance.

For two-story birdhouse
Cut a 5½×4½-inch bottom piece, two 5½×9¼-inch side pieces, one 7¼×4½-inch roof piece, one 7¼×5-inch roof piece, two 11¼×5-inch front/back pieces, and two ½×2½-inch perches from pine. Cut 45-degree angles to a center point along a 5-inch-long edge on both the front and back pieces.

Enlarge and trace star from pattern, *below.* Referring to pattern for placement, transfer star to front piece twice using carbon paper between pattern and wood. Cut out stars as for saltbox birdhouse, *left.*

Attach side pieces to bottom piece using glue and brads. Attach front and back pieces to bottom piece in same manner. Glue smaller roof piece in place, taking care to align top edge with front and back points; secure with brads. Glue and nail larger roof piece with top edge overlapping smaller roof piece. Glue and nail perches in place, one below each star hole.

Paint and sand entire piece as for saltbox birdhouse.

For small birdhouse
Cut a 3×5-inch bottom piece, two 2½×3¼-inch side pieces, one 4¾×3½-inch roof piece, one 4¾×3¼-inch roof piece, and two 3⅞×4¼-inch front/back pieces.

Enlarge and trace the small birdhouse pattern, *below,* onto tracing paper. Transfer pattern to the front and back pieces using carbon paper between pattern and wood. Cut front and back pieces according to pattern. Drill a ⅞-inch-diameter hole in the front piece as shown on the pattern.

Attach each side piece to front piece using glue and two brad nails. Attach back piece to side pieces in same manner. Glue smaller roof piece in place, taking care to align top edge with front and back points; secure with brads. Glue and nail larger roof piece, with top edge overlapping smaller roof piece. Apply a bead of glue along bottom edges of assembly; attach bottom piece and secure with brads.

Paint and sand entire piece as for other birdhouses.

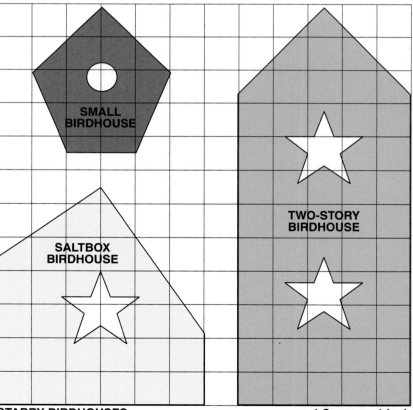

STARRY BIRDHOUSES   **1 Square = 1 Inch**

SMALL BIRDHOUSE

TWO-STORY BIRDHOUSE

SALTBOX BIRDHOUSE

Toast the Birds Trims

As shown on pages 30–31, finished trims are approximately 3 inches long.

MATERIALS

Cookie cutters in desired shapes
Tracing paper; lightweight cardboard
Sliced sandwich bread; paring knife
Thread or fine jute; tiny sticks

INSTRUCTIONS

For birdhouse shape, trace the pattern, *below,* onto tracing paper; cut out. Transfer pattern to cardboard and cut out.

Toast desired number of bread slices. Place cardboard pattern over toasted bread and trim bread using a paring knife. Use cookie cutters to cut other desired shapes.

Cut large holes in the centers of shapes, if desired; cut two large holes in the birdhouse shape. Cut a small hole at the top of each trim.

Thread jute or thread through top holes in trims and knot ends for hangers. Cut sticks into 1-inch lengths and poke in trims for perches, if desired.

TOAST THE BIRDS TRIM

Into the Woods Felt Ornaments

As shown on page 32, each ornament is 5×5 inches.

MATERIALS FOR ONE ORNAMENT

Tracing paper
6x6-inch piece of dark green felt
4¼x4¼-inch piece of check or plaid
fabric in desired country colors
4¼x4¼-inch piece of fusible web
5x9-inch piece of black felt
Scrap of gold felt (for wolf)
4x4-inch piece of fleece
Cotton embroidery floss: black and
color to match check or plaid fabric

INSTRUCTIONS

Enlarge and trace ornament pattern and desired full-size animal pattern, *page 38,* onto tracing paper; cut out. Cut ornament pattern from green felt and animal from black felt. Also from black felt, cut a 4¼x4¼-inch square backing piece and a ½×4½-inch hanging loop strip. If using wolf design, cut moon from gold felt.

Center the fusible web on the dark green felt; place the check or plaid fabric square atop the web. Following the manufacturer's instructions for fusible web, fuse the fabric to the felt. Using two plies of matching embroidery floss, sew the fabric to the felt with a running stitch (see *page 38*) around the perimeter, ⅛ inch from the edges.

Center the fleece square on the back of the ornament, cover with black felt backing piece, and whipstitch the backing to dark green felt.

Position the animal diagonally on the ornament front and pin in place. Appliqué-stitch, *page 40,* the ornament in place, using two plies of black floss and stitching through all of the layers. Hand-quilt around the animal using two plies of floss in a color that matches the fabric.

For hanging loop, join the ends of the strip; whipstitch the ends to the back of ornament at top corner.

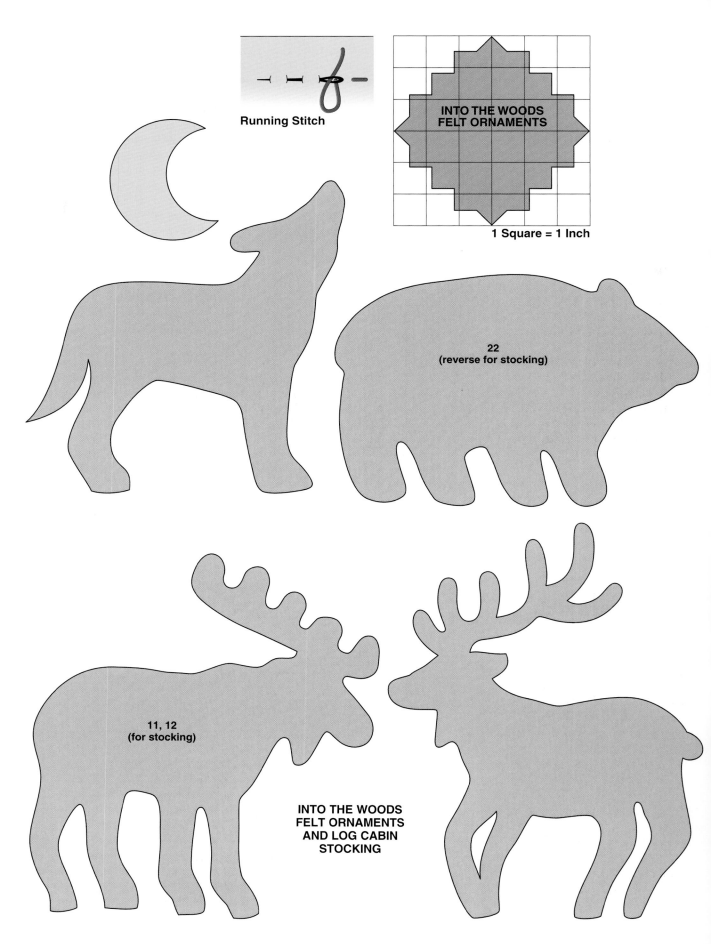

Running Stitch

INTO THE WOODS
FELT ORNAMENTS

1 Square = 1 Inch

22
(reverse for stocking)

11, 12
(for stocking)

INTO THE WOODS
FELT ORNAMENTS
AND LOG CABIN
STOCKING

Log Cabin Stocking

As shown on page 33, stocking is 18½×10½ inches.

MATERIALS
Tracing paper
½ yard of black felt; ½ yard of brown felt
6x9-inch piece *each* **of navy blue solid, green print, brown-and-white check, red-and-tan check, blue and tan check, black-and-brown check, red plaid, and blue print cotton fabrics**
3x9-inch piece of red print cotton fabric
6x6-inch piece *each* **of gold felt, kelly green felt, dark red felt, and dark green felt**
Scrap *each* **of white and lavender felt**
Paper-backed double-sided fusible adhesive; pins
Cotton embroidery floss in colors to match felt, plus navy blue
Tapestry needle; embroidery scissors

INSTRUCTIONS
Trace full-size patterns, *pages 40 and 38*, onto tracing paper; cut out. Enlarge stocking outline and shapes 1–3 and 6–10, *right*, onto tracing paper and cut out. Cut stocking front from black felt and stocking back from brown felt. Following manufacturer's instructions, fuse paper-backed adhesive to back of cotton fabric (not felt) pieces.

Cut piece 1 from navy blue solid; cut pieces 2 and 3 from green print; cut piece 6 from brown-and-white check; cut piece 8 from red-and-tan check; cut piece 7 from blue-and-tan check; cut piece 9 from black-and-brown check; cut piece 10 from red plaid; cut piece 5 from blue print; and cut piece 4 from red print.

Cut pieces 11, 12, 17, 22, and 27 from remaining black felt. Cut pieces 13, 14, 15, 23, 24, and 25 from gold felt; cut piece 16 from kelly green felt; cut piece 21 from dark red felt; cut piece 26 from dark green felt; cut pieces 18 and 20 from white felt; and cut piece 19 from lavender felt.

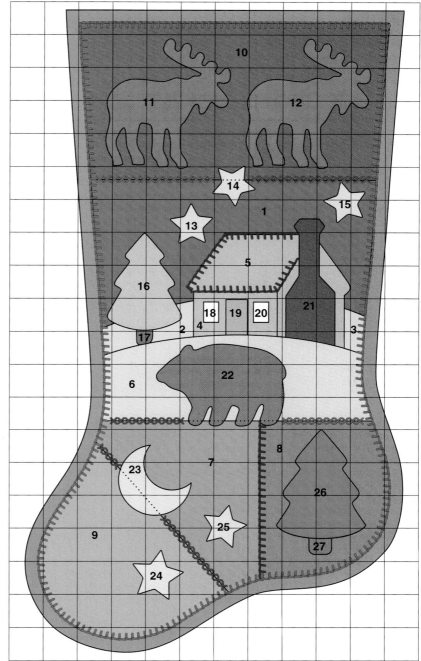

LOG CABIN STOCKING   **1 Square = 1 Inch**

Referring to diagram, *above*, remove paper backing from piece 1 and fuse in place on stocking front. Repeat with pieces 2–10 in numerical sequence. Use a blanket stitch (see stitches on *page 40*) around piece 5.

Pin felt pieces 11 and 12 in place. Sew pieces to stocking front using appliqué stitch and one ply of matching floss. In same manner, pin and stitch pieces 13 through 27.

Add cross-stitches and blanket stitches as shown on diagram, using desired colors. Use three plies of floss to stitch between major patches of fabric, around roof, and around outer edge of stocking.

Sew stocking front to back using black floss and a running stitch, *page 38*, ⅜ inch from edge.

Cut a zigzag pattern in the outer edge of black felt stocking front. Refer to photograph on *page 33* as a guide.

Cut three ½×9-inch strips from brown felt; braid strips. Stitch ends to stocking back for hanging loop.

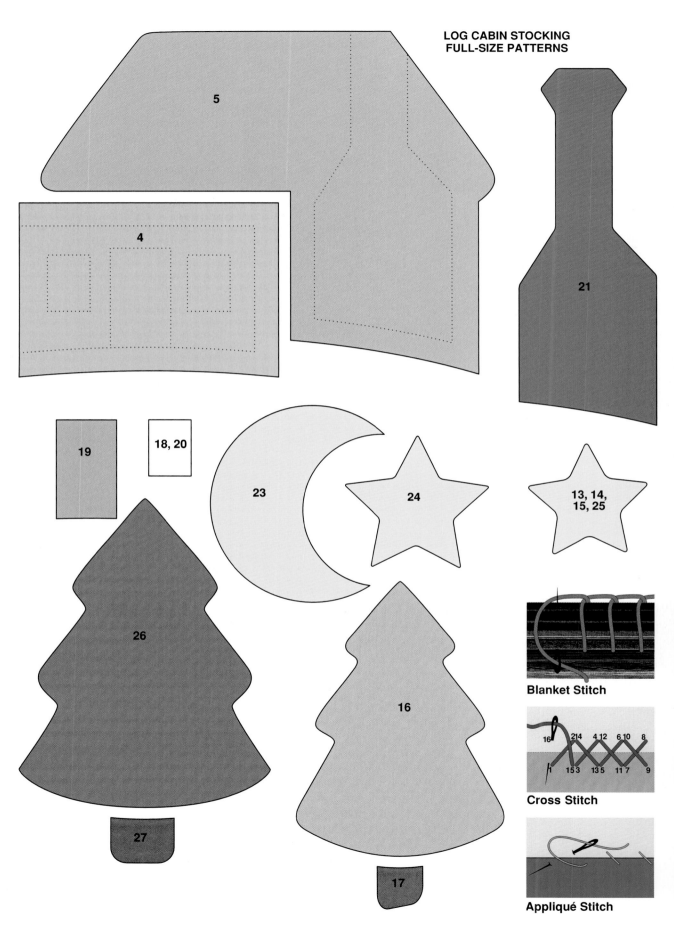

LOG CABIN STOCKING
FULL-SIZE PATTERNS

5

4

21

19

18, 20

23

24

13, 14,
15, 25

26

16

27

17

Blanket Stitch

Cross Stitch

Appliqué Stitch

40

Gather the materials you need to create this bird-loving wreath. Our wreath uses rose hips, but you can substitute elderberry, bayberry, or juniper branches.

Nature's Own Fruit Wreath

As shown on page 34, wreath is approximately 24 inches in diameter.

MATERIALS
Grapevine wreath; garden clippers
Hemlock boughs; craft wire
Rose hips or elderberry, bayberry,
    or juniper branches; knife
Several navel oranges; florist's picks

INSTRUCTIONS
Gather the materials to make wreath as shown in Step 1, *left.*

   Cut and attach greens to wreath (see Step 2, *below left*). Continue wiring hemlock and rose hips until the grapevine is not visible.

   Cut and arrange oranges as shown in Step 3, *below.* Secure a florist's pick into each orange section, pushing the other end into the grapevine wreath.

Cut hemlock greens into small pieces, wiring stems onto grapevine wreath. Pull wire taut to keep greens in place. Wire sprigs of rose hips over the hemlock.

Cut oranges in halves, quarters, and slices, and position the pieces on the wreath in an eye-pleasing design. Birds will eat only cut oranges, so place the fruit side facing out.

Nature Lover's Cross-Stitch

As shown on page 35.

MATERIALS

FABRIC
18x22-inch piece of 28-count light blue Jobelan

FLOSS
Cotton embroidery floss in colors listed in key

SUPPLIES
Embroidery hoop; needle; mat; frame

INSTRUCTIONS

Find center of chart, *pages 42–43,* and the center of the fabric; begin stitching there.

Use two plies of floss to work all cross-stitches over two threads of fabric. Work blended needle stitches as indicated in key. Work half cross-stitches, straight stitches, French knots, and lazy daisy stitches using two plies. Backstitch using one ply. Attach beads using one ply of matching floss.

Press the stitchery from the back. Mat and frame as desired.

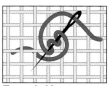

French Knot

Lazy Daisy Stitch

NATURE LOVER'S CROSS-STITCH

Anchor		DMC
387	△	Ecru
002	•	000 White
1025	◈	347 Salmon
010	◎	351 Light coral
009	⟋	352 Pale coral
1005	♥	498 Christmas red
683	◆	500 Deep blue green
1042	✳	504 Pale blue green
1041	#	535 Ash gray
280	⊠	581 True moss green
886	—	677 Old gold
256	⟍	704 Chartreuse
302	☆	743 Yellow
1012	♡	754 Medium peach
309	★	781 Topaz
307	◉	783 Christmas gold
013	⊕	817 Deep coral
257	+	905 Parrot green
848	◫	927 Gray blue
268	⋈	937 Pine green
1011	⊓	948 Light peach
246	●	986 Forest green
391	□	3033 Pale mocha
888	×	3045 Yellow beige
382	■	3371 Black brown
1050	▲	3781 Dark mocha
851	◤	3808 Deep turquoise
168	∿	3810 True turquoise
877	⊖	3815 Celadon green
278	△	3819 Light moss green
306	▽	3820 Dark straw
874	‖	3822 Light straw
	✳	5282 Light gold metallic

BLENDED NEEDLE

944	◙	869 Hazel (1X) and
888		3045 Yellow beige (1X)
120	◇	3747 Periwinkle (1X) and
		025 Kreinik gray blending filament (1X)
002	⊡	000 White (1X) and
		032 Kreinik pearl blending filament (1X)

HALF CROSS-STITCH

979	⟋	312 Navy

Anchor		DMC	
BACKSTITCH			
401	⟋	413	Pewter – Christmas roses and doves
683	⟋	500	Blue green – holly, leaves, and letters
043	⟋	815	Garnet – border
360	⟋	898	Coffee brown – ribbon, rabbits, berries, manger, and poinsettias
1011	⟋	948	Light peach – berry highlights
382	⟋	3371	Black brown – pine trees
	⟋	5282	Light gold metallic – border, evergreen trees and manger
	⟋	025	Krienik gray blending filament – trees snow

STRAIGHT STITCH

002	⟋	000	White – stars
401	⟋	413	Pewter – Christmas roses
360	⟋	898	Coffee brown – rabbit fur
268	⟋	937	Pine green – centers of lazy daisy stitches
851	⟋	3808	Deep turquoise – pine boughs
	⟋	5282	Light gold metallic – star

FRENCH KNOT

387	○		Ecru – doves' eyes, rabbits' eyes
002	◦	000	White – star centers
302	○	743	Yellow – Christmas rose centers
043	●	815	Garnet – tiny bushes by rabbits
1002	◦	977	Golden brown – Christmas rose centers and poinsettia centers
382	●	3371	Black brown – berry tips

LAZY DAISY

280	₀	581	True moss green – mistletoe

MILL HILL GLASS BEADS

	○	00561	Ice green seed bead – inner border
	○	00557	Gold seed bead – star
	○	03054	Cream antique seed bead – mistletoe berries

Stitch count: *164 high x 204 wide*

Finished design sizes:
28-count fabric – 11³/₄ x 14¹/₂ inches
22-count fabric – 15 x 18¹/₂ inches
36-count fabric – 9¹/₈ x 11³/₈ inches

SIMPLE gifts

There's always enough time to make that perfect gift for a close friend and it doesn't need to take hours and hours. We've collected some quick-to-make gifts that will be just right for that special someone on your Christmas list.

family memory CANDLES

Family Christmas cards or photo greetings can be enjoyed all year long by carefully wrapping photocopies of them around a pillar candle. We've trimmed our candles with sequins and jingle bells. Instructions are on page 55.

Design: Carol Dahlstrom

playful felt

MITTENS

A mitten cut from felt becomes a festive holder for silverware—and a perfect gift for a little one. Embellished with blanket stitches, this tiny mitten can also hold other holiday surprises. Full-size patterns and instructions are on page 55.

Design: Karen Taylor

christmas
KITCHEN
trims

Flea market finds suitable for the kitchen take on a new life when decorated with evergreen and red berries. We've added cinnamon sticks to our tiny arrangement, too. Instructions are on page 56.

Design: Donna Chesnut

simple
BUTTON
snowman

Tiny white buttons resemble glistening snow, bringing our snowman to life. We've tied on a jaunty ribbon scarf and stacked buttons for a hat, giving him personality plus. Instructions are on page 56.

Design: Donna Chesnut

stars in the
CHIMNEY
centerpiece

Simple star shapes etched into a hurricane lamp create a stunning centerpiece when combined with a purple candle. Perfect for a hostess gift (or to display yourself), we've surrounded our centerpiece with greens and sparkling beads. Instructions are on page 56.

Design: Phyllis Dunstan

gingerbread
BABIES

These little gingerbread babies are sure to be everyone's favorites. Made from flannel and filled with birdseed, these posable friends will please young and old alike. Full-size patterns and instructions are on pages 57–58.

Design: Karen Taylor

Paper bags with handles become favorite wraps when you add a little felt, buttons, and a few quick stitches. We've filled our bags with candles to give, but they can hold all kinds of treats. Full-size patterns and instructions are on pages 58–59.

Design: Phyllis Dobbs

scribbles GOODY bags

Cellophane corsage bags make surprisingly easy goody holders. We used paint pens to personalize and embellish our bags, then filled them with nuts and candies. Instructions are on page 60.

Design: Carol Dahlstrom

Family Memory Candles

As shown on page 46.

Large pillar candle
Photocopied pictures from
    Christmas cards
½ yard of sequins-by-the-yard
½-inch straight pins
Gold cording and jingle bells (optional)

INSTRUCTIONS

Measure around the candle. Cut the photocopied picture 1 inch wider than the circumference of the candle.

Wrap a picture around each candle, overlapping the sides and making sure the paper is at least 2 to 3 inches below the candle top; pin in place. In the same manner, pin the sequins around the top of each photo. Finish by tying gold cording hung with jingle bells into a bow, if desired. *(Caution: Be sure that the candle burns into the middle of the pillar. Do not let the candle burn past the paper top edge.)*

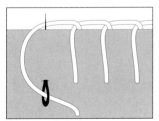

Blanket Stitch

Playful Felt Mittens

As shown on page 47, mitten measures 6¼×4 inches.

MATERIALS FOR ONE MITTEN
Tracing paper
9x12-inch piece of felt in
    desired color
3x3-inch piece of white felt
White cotton embroidery floss
Tapestry needle
Two 1x3-inch strips of white fleece
Five ½-inch-diameter buttons
Two ⅜-inch-diameter silver
    jingle bells

INSTRUCTIONS

Trace mitten and star patterns, *below*, onto tracing paper; cut out. Cut two mitten pieces from colored felt and one star from white felt. Sew the star to one mitten as shown in photograph, *page 47*, using two plies of white floss and small straight stitches.

Sew mitten pieces together, wrong sides facing, using six plies of floss and the blanket stitch (see diagram, *below*). Leave wrist edges open.

Glue fleece strip to the wrist edges. Glue button to tip of thumb; glue four buttons around curved edge of mitten.

Tack jingle bell to each side of mitten at fleece edge. Add floss loop at wrist edge for hanging.

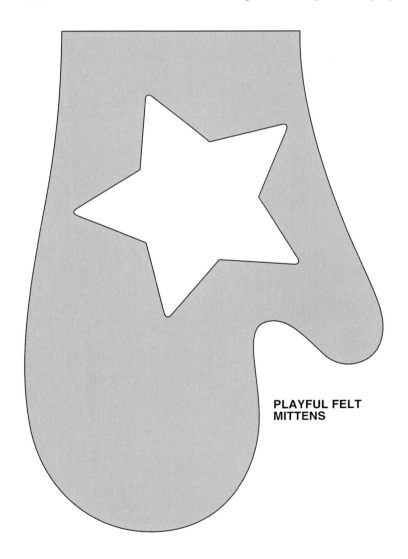

PLAYFUL FELT MITTENS

Christmas Kitchen Trims

As shown on page 48, finished trim is 9 inches high.

MATERIALS

Old kitchen grater or other old utensil; hot-glue gun; hot glue
Spanish moss; artificial greens
Cinnamon sticks; pinecones
Red berries
Spray-on artificial snow (optional)
¼-inch-wide plaid ribbon scrap

INSTRUCTIONS

Glue a small bunch of Spanish moss to the front of the grater. Add small pieces of greens, cinnamon sticks, pinecones, and berries; glue in place.

Spray a light coating of artificial snow over the front of the decorated grater, if desired. Tie ribbon into a bow on the handle.

Button Snowman

As shown on page 49, snowman stands 10½ inches tall.

MATERIALS

4-inch-diameter plastic foam ball, 3-inch-diameter plastic foam ball, and a 2-inch-diameter plastic foam ball
Assorted white buttons, up to 1 inch in diameter
2-inch black button
Five 1- or 1½-inch-diameter black buttons or checkers
Five ½-inch-diameter black buttons
¼-inch-diameter black button
Hot-glue gun; hot glue
⅛-inch-diameter dowel
Black cotton embroidery floss; needle
3 small twigs; round toothpick
Orange acrylic paint
Small paintbrush
Small bunch of natural broom straw, cut to 7 inches long
Fine gauge wire; 24 inches of 1½-inch-wide red plaid ribbon
6-inch-diameter plastic foam circle

INSTRUCTIONS

Hot glue enough white buttons to each plastic foam ball to cover, reserving two ¼-inch four-hole white buttons for eyes. Stack and glue checkers or larger black buttons in order of size to make top hat. Glue hat to top of 2-inch-diameter ball.

Cut dowel into two 2-inch-long pieces. Use dowels to connect the balls in a snowman configuration. Use glue as necessary. Push twig arms into place on medium-size ball. Glue ½-inch-diameter black buttons down front as shown in photograph, *above.*

Sew a floss X through holes in white eye buttons; glue in place on face. Glue ¼-inch-diameter black button to face for mouth. Paint a toothpick orange; push it into the face for a nose.

For broom, wire broom straw around base of remaining twig. Hot-glue broom handle to one arm.

Wrap and tie ribbon around neck for scarf. Glue completed snowman to circular plastic foam base.

Chimney Centerpiece

As shown on page 50, chimney is 8 inches tall.

MATERIALS

White vinegar; hurricane lamp
¼-inch-wide masking tape
Burnishing tool (wooden orange stick or tongue depressor)
Armour glass etching cream
Paintbrush; plastic gloves
Adhesive star stickers in two sizes or contact paper
Tulip Slick paint in any color

INSTRUCTIONS

Wash the hurricane lamp with white vinegar to remove any fingerprints; let dry.

Wrap a strip of masking tape around the bottom of the hurricane 1¼ inches up from the bottom edge. Fill the section below the tape with vertical strips of masking tape placed ¼ inch apart. Rub all tape edges with the burnishing tool.

Follow the manufacturer's directions on the etching cream jar to etch glass. Wear plastic gloves when washing the cream off.

Clean off all fingerprints with white vinegar.

To etch the stars, remove the stars from the strip and place on waxed paper. Peel the backing off the leftover portion, creating a star stencil, and stick this onto the hurricane lamp. Repeat with more stars, using both sizes of stars and placing them randomly around the hurricane lamp. Rub down the edges with the burnishing tool. *(Note: If the star points are too close to the edge of the paper, surround the star stencil with strips of masking tape.)* If desired, cut the star shapes from squares of contact paper instead of using purchased star stickers.

Etch all of the star stencils. Wearing plastic gloves, wash the etching cream off with warm water.

Use the paint to make dots between the stripes at the bottom edge of the hurricane lamp.

Gingerbread Babies

As shown on page 51, gingerbread babies measure 9×7 inches.

MATERIALS FOR TWO BABIES
Tracing paper
⅓ yard of tan flannel
Thread to match fabric
Birdseed
Small funnel
Shiny paint pens: white, black, red, and green

INSTRUCTIONS
Trace the pattern, *page 57*, onto tracing paper; cut out. Cut four body pieces from flannel.

With right sides facing, sew the body pieces together in pairs, using ¼-inch seam allowances. Leave a 2-inch-long opening along an inner leg seam for stuffing. Turn each gingerbread baby right side out. Using funnel, fill each body with birdseed; sew the openings closed.

Outline each body front with white paint pen to resemble piped frosting. Add white eyebrows, noses, and mouths. Use black paint pen to make oval eyes. Finish decorating the gingerbread babies with red and green paint pens as desired, using the pattern, *page 57,* and the photograph, *above,* for ideas.

Country Christmas Paper Bags

As shown on pages 52–53, designs measure between 5 and 5½ inches high.

MATERIALS FOR SET OF THREE BAGS
Tracing paper
Three 5¼x8¼-inch craft paper bags
Three 9x12-inch sheets of felt: white, red, and green
Cotton embroidery floss in desired colors
Assorted buttons: red, green, cream, taupe, and blue
Black Mill Hill pebble beads
No. 22 chenille needle or embroidery needle
White crafts glue; pencil

INSTRUCTIONS
Trace patterns, *above and opposite,* onto tracing paper; cut out. Cut one of each shape from felt.

Lay felt shapes on bags to determine placement of words as indicated on patterns. Lightly pencil the words on the bags. Remove felt shapes. Backstitch words using three plies of floss as indicated on patterns. Glue felt shapes on bags; let dry.

Lightly draw the snowman's arms. Stitch the arms with long stitches using six plies of brown floss. Sew on black beads for the snowman's buttons and eyes. Stitch a mouth using three plies of red floss.

Stitch buttons on the star, tree, and all three bags, referring to photograph, *pages 52–53.* Stitch around the edges of the felt shapes using three plies of floss and straight stitches in random lengths.

SEASONS
GREETINGS

PEACE

JOY

LOVE

Scribbles Goody Bags

As shown on page 54.

MATERIALS FOR ONE GOODY BAG
Two cellophane corsage bags
    (available at florist supply stores)
White typing paper
Paint pens in various colors
Candies, nuts, or other goodies to eat
Rubber bands
Ribbon

INSTRUCTIONS
Lay corsage bag flat on work
surface and insert paper between
the layers so the bag remains flat.
Using examples, *right*, as a guide,
draw dots, squiggles, and lines over
the front of the corsage bag using
paint pens. Add a name, if desired.
Allow the paint to dry.

Fill an undecorated bag with
goodies to desired fullness; tie with
a rubber band. Put the filled bag into
the decorated bag and tie closed
with ribbon.

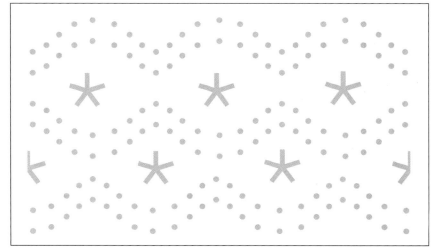

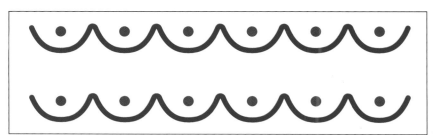

make a
JOYFUL
noise

Whether you are sharing your gift of
music by performing at Christmastime
or simply enjoying the sounds of the
season, the beauty of carols and
other holiday songs is surely one of
the loveliest gifts of all. In this
chapter we offer ideas for sharing
the gift of music.

music
ENSEMBLE
evergreen

Wrap your tree in pleasing notes and golden instruments for a most harmonious tree. For a closer look at the trims, see the next page.

Design: Donna Chesnut

golden musical
INSTRUMENTS

Harps, trumpets, horns, violins, and saxophones—they all combine to make beautiful music and elegant ornaments for your tree. Painted metallic gold, the trims have details made from tiny dowels. Our Wooden Melody Garland has a staff of golden cord. Instructions are on pages 69–71.

Design: Donna Chesnut

SINGING
star ornaments

Folded paper and musical notes combine to make these simple yet stunning tree ornaments. String the stars into a garland or let them hang alone for a striking effect. Instructions and patterns are on pages 71–72.

Design: Phyllis Dunstan

christmas
CAROL
packages

Pleasing the musicians on your list with harmonious wrapping paper is as easy as ABC when you recycle sheet music. Use clear tape to piece the paper together for larger gifts and tie with a golden ribbon bow.

Design: Carol Dahlstrom

vintage music
CASES

A tired old suitcase will sing again covered with castaway vintage music. We've chosen Christmas carols to decoupage the suitcase, which we lined in red velvet. Fill this elegant piece with greens, cards, gifts, or favorite musical instruments. Instructions are on page 72.

Design: Carol Dahlstrom and Alice Wetzel

perfect harmony
TABLETOP

Create a holiday tabletop your favorite music lovers will always remember. We began by using a glitter paint pen to draw the staff and notes on a cream-color place mat. Then we used an old record as a charger and placed our painted Perfect Harmony Keyboard Plate atop this fun LP. Our Musical Note Bar Cookies and Drummer Boy Cookies add the finishing touch. Recipes and instructions are on page 73.

Designs: Carol Dahlstrom

music lover's
GIFT BASKET

For that serious music devotee on your list, fill a basket with musical gifts. We've included compact discs, cassette tapes, a tiny cassette tape player—even a collectible record. What better way to be in tune with the season!

Design: Carol Dahlstrom

Golden Musical Instruments

As shown on pages 62–63, instruments vary from 2½×6½ to 4½×8 inches.

MATERIALS FOR ONE SET OF FIVE
Tracing paper
12x18-inch piece of ¼-inch plywood
Bandsaw; drill; ⅛-inch drill bit
Sandpaper
1/16-inch-diameter dowel (for harp and violin)
⅛-inch-diameter dowel (for French horn, trumpet, and saxophone)
Utility scissors
Crafts glue *or* hot-glue gun and hot glue
Gold spray paint
Five 8-inch-long pieces of gold metallic rattail cord

INSTRUCTIONS
Trace the instrument patterns, *below* and *page 70*, onto tracing paper; cut out. Draw around the patterns on plywood; transfer dots. Cut out using a bandsaw. Drill ⅛-inch holes at dots. Sand pieces lightly.

Cut dowels into pieces using dowel lines marked on patterns as guides. Glue the dowel pieces onto the instruments as shown on the patterns.

Spray all pieces gold; allow to dry. Tie gold cord through the holes into hanging loops.

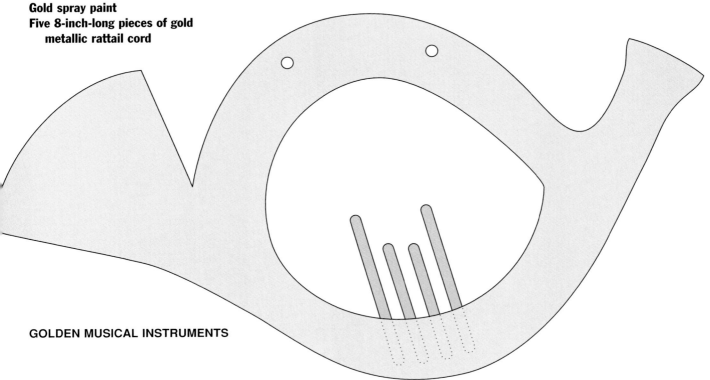

GOLDEN MUSICAL INSTRUMENTS

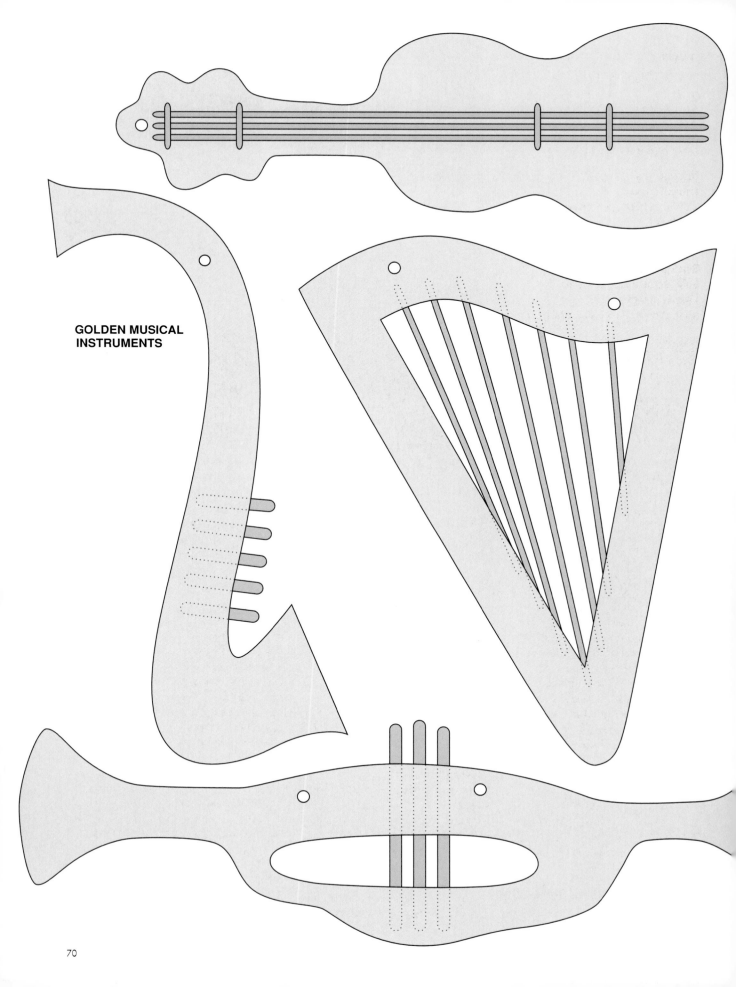

GOLDEN MUSICAL
INSTRUMENTS

Wooden Melody Garland

As shown on pages 62–63, finished garland is approximately 8 feet long.

MATERIALS
Tracing paper
1x2-foot sheet of ¼-inch plywood
Bandsaw
Sandpaper
Drill; ⅛-inch drill bit
Black acrylic spray paint
Gold metallic acrylic paint
½-inch paintbrush
45 feet of gold metallic rattail cord

INSTRUCTIONS
Trace musical note pattern, *right*, onto tracing paper; cut out. Draw around pattern on plywood seven times; transfer dots for holes.

Cut out notes using a bandsaw; sand lightly. Drill ⅛-inch holes at the dots.

Spray notes black. When dry, brush edges lightly with gold and allow to dry.

Cut cord into 9-foot-long pieces. Beginning with first musical note right side up, thread cord piece in and out the top sets of horizontal holes. Thread a second cord piece through the second set of holes in same manner. Repeat, with the remaining three cord pieces. Next, turn a second note upside down so the round part is at the top and thread it onto the cord pieces in the same manner, sliding on the second note until it is 10 inches from first. Continue threading notes onto cords in the same manner, alternating positions. After all notes are threaded, spaced 10 inches apart, knot cord ends together, and trim.

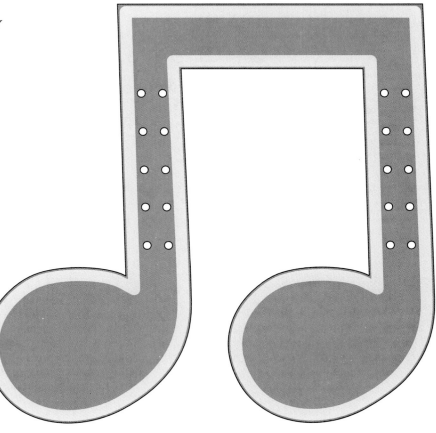

Singing Star Ornaments

As shown on page 64, stars vary from 5½×5½ to 9×9 inches.

MATERIALS FOR ONE STAR
Page of sheet music
Tracing paper
Lightweight cardboard; ruler
Large sewing needle
Knitting needle *or* other scoring stylus
FOR ORNAMENTS
Fine gold cord; 6mm gold beads
FOR GARLAND
⅛-inch hole punch
Red crochet thread; small gold bells

INSTRUCTIONS
Trace the star patterns, *page 72*, onto tracing paper; cut out. *Note: There are three sizes given.* Draw around the patterns on cardboard, making a template for each star; cut out. Trace around the templates onto sheet music, tracing the number of stars desired; cut out stars.

Poke a small hole in the center of the star using a needle. Referring to pattern, use the scoring stylus and ruler to score the solid lines on the right side of each star. Turn the star over; score the broken lines.

Fold each point on the line scored on the front. Turn each star over and fold on the lines scored on back.

For ornaments, thread needle with fine gold cord; pull through tip of one point. Remove needle and thread ends of cord through one or two gold beads. Knot ends together to make a hanging loop.

To make a garland, randomly arrange a row of stars in various sizes, overlapping points. Cut tips off overlapping points. Punch holes in trimmed tips. Using 8-inch-long pieces of crochet thread, tie star tips together through holes, slipping a bell onto one of the thread ends before tying. Pull points together until they touch; knot.

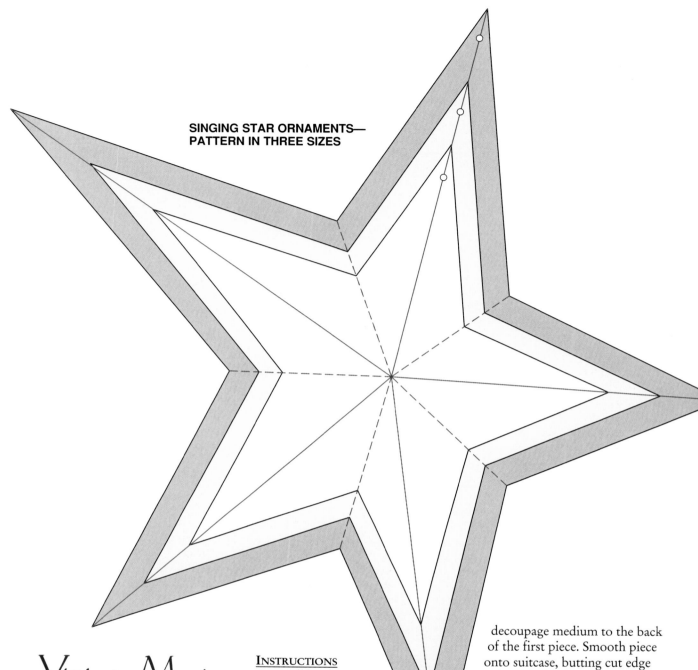

**SINGING STAR ORNAMENTS—
PATTERN IN THREE SIZES**

Vintage Music Cases

As shown on page 65.

MATERIALS
**Old suitcase with metal hardware and
leather trim; black acrylic paint**
Gold metallic spray paint
Artists' paintbrushes: 1- and ½-inch flat
Paintbrushes: 2- and 3-inches-wide
**Old sheet music printed on medium
to thick paper stock**
Scissors *or* crafts knife
Mod Podge decoupage medium

INSTRUCTIONS

Spray all hardware gold. Allow some overspray onto body of suitcase or trim if necessary to get maximum coverage; let dry.

Paint leather trim black, working carefully around hardware. In addition, paint any visible inside edges. Allow paint to dry.

Plan general placement of music, creating a random pattern by positioning music at different angles. Begin next to black trim. Using scissors or knife, cut angled pieces to fit. Apply a thin coat of decoupage medium to the back of the first piece. Smooth piece onto suitcase, butting cut edge against black trim. Smooth out wrinkles. When working around odd-shaped trim or hardware, lap music over hardware, press firmly along edges, allow to dry, and trim away overlap with knife. Continue applying pieces of sheet music, layering as desired and working toward center. If suitcase surface is textured, it may help to brush medium onto suitcase before applying sheet music.

When music is dry, spread two coats of decoupage medium over the entire suitcase, avoiding the hardware and letting it dry between coats.

Musical Note Bar Cookies

As shown on page 66.

INGREDIENTS

1¼ cups all-purpose flour
1 cup sifted powdered sugar
½ cup unsweetened cocoa powder
¼ teaspoon baking soda
¾ cup butter
1 tablespoon instant coffee crystals
1 8-ounce package cream cheese, softened
1 14-ounce can sweetened condensed milk (1¼ cups)
2 eggs
    Powdered sugar or chocolate frosting tinted black with paste food coloring

METHOD

Stir together flour, powdered sugar, cocoa powder, and baking soda. With a pastry blender or fork, cut in butter till mixture resembles coarse crumbs; press into the bottom of a foil-lined 13×9×2-inch baking pan. Bake in a 350° oven for 15 minutes.

Meanwhile, dissolve coffee crystals in 1 tablespoon hot water; set aside. Beat cream cheese in a large mixing bowl with an electric mixer till fluffy. Gradually beat in sweetened condensed milk. Add coffee mixture and eggs; beat on low speed just till combined. Pour over crust. Bake in a 350° oven for 20 minutes or till set. Cool on a wire rack. Cover and chill. Use foil to lift cookies carefully out of pan. If desired, trim edges. Cut into bars. Sprinkle with powdered sugar (over a doily for lacy effect) or pipe black frosting in the shape of musical notes,

treble clef, or treble staff.* Makes 32.
Use a small round writing tip, such as Wilton decorating tip No. 2 or No. 3, to pipe notes or clef sign.

Drummer Boy Cookies

As shown on page 66.

INGREDIENTS

⅓ cup butter
⅓ cup shortening
¾ cup packed brown sugar
1 teaspoon baking powder
½ teaspoon ground cinnamon
¼ teaspoon salt
1 egg
1 tablespoon milk
½ teaspoon vanilla
1¾ cups all-purpose flour
¼ cup whole wheat flour
    Desired frosting

METHOD

Beat butter and shortening in a mixing bowl with an electric mixer on medium to high speed for 30 seconds. Add brown sugar, baking powder, cinnamon, and salt; beat till combined. Beat egg, milk, and vanilla into sugar mixture. Beat in as much of the all-purpose flour as you can with the mixer. Stir in remaining all-purpose flour and whole wheat flour with a wooden spoon. Divide dough in half. Cover and chill about 3 hours or till easy to handle.

Roll each half of dough ⅛ inch thick on a lightly floured surface.

Cut into 2½-inch to 3-inch rounds with cookie cutter dipped in flour. With a sharp knife, cut off opposite edges of rounds to make drum shapes. Place cutouts 1 inch apart on ungreased cookie sheets.

Bake in a 375° oven for 7 to 8 minutes or till edges are firm. Cool on cookie sheets for 1 minute. Remove from cookie sheets and cool on wire racks. Decorate with desired frosting to look like drums. Makes about 40.

Perfect Harmony Keyboard Plate

As shown on pages 66–67.

MATERIALS

Clear plate in desired size
Paint designed for decorating glass or china: black and white
Masking tape; X-Acto knife
Small paintbrush

INSTRUCTIONS

On the underside of plate, mask off areas to be painted. Using the white paint, paint the white keys of the keyboard first using the photograph, *pages 66–67,* as a guide. Allow to dry. Paint the black keys of the keyboard; let dry. Remove the tape. Follow the manufacturer's instructions for curing paint.

Perfect Harmony Place Mat

As shown on pages 66–67.

MATERIALS

Purchased place mat
Gold glitter paint pen

INSTRUCTIONS

Looking at a musical score for guidance, draw musical staffs, treble and bass clef signs, and musical notes as desired using paint pen. Allow the paint to dry.

a SEASON of giving

Gift giving—a joy and an art—is as ageless as time itself. Whether given from the tiniest hand from child to mother or as a gesture of kindness friend to friend, the art of giving gifts finds its most glorious season at Christmastime.

Christmas gift-giving originated when the Three Kings brought gifts to the baby Jesus—celebrating God's gift to the world. Agreeing that the star heralded the coming of a Savior in Israel, three Wise Men who were philosophers and astrologers from the east, were drawn to Bethlehem. The rich Magi—Gaspar, Melchior, and Balthazar—followed the star to the quaint stable where they found Mary and the Baby. While artwork throughout history showed different numbers of Wise Men, these three individuals became the accepted trio in the 6th century.

After worshiping the newborn Messiah and hailing him as the "King of Israel" and "Prince of Peace," the Magi offered the Babe their exotic treasures of gold, frankincense, and myrrh.

The gold, a valuable metal, was said to symbolize love or Christ as King of the world. The sweet spice, frankincense, stood for prayer or Christ as the King of Heaven. A symbol of Christ's approaching suffering and sacrifice, was myrrh, an aromatic resin found in the bark of thorny African trees.

It is said that these gift-bearing Kings represented all of humanity. The King of Pamphlia, Melchior, was represented as an old man with white hair and a long beard. He offered the gold to the newborn King. Young Gaspar, King of

CHRISTMAS GREETING

May He whose gifts are
blessings true
At Christmastide be near
to you

Chaldaea, presented his gift of frankincense—the homage due to Divinity. And the third King, Balthazar, was the King of Ethiopia. This bearded black King offered myrrh to the baby Jesus.

A 15th century artist, Jacobus de Voragine, created detailed manuscript illuminations which depict the birth of the Christ Child and the magical visit of the Three Kings. His works suggested that the gold would lessen Mary's poverty, the frankincense would ward off odors at the stable, and the myrrh would prevent vermin from inhabiting the manger area.

As the story of the Magi was passed from generation to generation, the story transcended into folklore and the Three Kings were said to be responsible for giving gifts to good children. This day is known as Three Kings Day which is celebrated on January 6, the Epiphany.

Today, as we observe the birth of Christ and the adoration of the Magi, we celebrate the blessed event with our family and friends through holiday gatherings and the giving of Christmas presents.

Before the 1800s, Christmas gift-giving was not influenced commercially. Gifts that were exchanged were usually fine food and drink given by landlords to their subservients.

This general celebration of gift giving quickly reached into the family unit. However, these gifts were to represent personal sentiments offered to family members, not food and drink offered because of obligation.

Nearly all family-given presents were homemade, touting the talents

of the maker. Whether lovingly sewn, proudly carved, or otherwise made by hand, these Christmas gifts were dearly cherished by whomever received them.

Once this gift-giving tradition was honored by most families throughout the United States, merchants began to produce and advertise an array of Christmas presents created for children. Shotguns, writing slates, dolls, drums, whistles, and firecrackers were only some of the toys that started appearing. Handmade gifts were highly discouraged in newspaper advertisements and soon became less fashionable.

Toys and books for children became the bulk of the manufactured Christmas presents in the early 1800s. Readily available and priced between 6 and 40 cents each, books were the most popular gifts for children. These books could have been bibles, storybooks, or books that would help teach children to read and write.

Noting the popularity of children's books, soon ornate books emerged that were written about Christmas itself—in the form of essays, stories, and poetry—and often accompanied by pictures capturing the warmth and tradition of the season. These gift books grew to cover all kinds of subjects and were available in a wide range of prices. There were presentation plates (a "to" and "from" label) within the cover so the gift book would have a personal touch.

Bibles became another keepsake to be given away at Christmastime. Coming in a variety of sizes, styles, and prices, bibles were produced for children and adults alike. Other popular gifts of the early 1800s were hymn books, sugarplums, cakes, apples, dolls, nuts, and clothes.

Before long, merchants realized they could broaden their target audience. Soon, women's jewelry and other fine gift objects began appearing in stores throughout the Christmas season. During this period, men were not perceived as appropriate recipients of commercial Christmas presents.

As the newspaper advertisements for Christmas gifts multiplied and more and more products became available, some people began to criticize the usefulness of many of the gifts and challenged whether these gifts were a waste of money. Some even felt that purchasing gifts was a tedious task and that trying to decide what to buy was a stressful undertaking.

But the tradition boomed on. Aggressive and sophisticated advertising appeared in newspapers earlier and earlier in December.

In the 1840s it wasn't unusual to see special supplements emphasizing the choices available and encouraging spending—even if it was a time of economic depression.

It was during this time that Santa Claus began to appear frequently in these newspaper advertisements. Newspapers even suggested that he be given a copy of the ads in order to help him select gifts for his long-awaited Christmas Eve voyage.

Confectioners, trying to increase their business, sometimes advertised that their goods could be purchased for less than the cost of a gift. In 1840 they started making "mammoth cakes" to display in their shop windows.

The idea caught on and the competition brought about fruitcakes that weighed up to 1,000 pounds and could be bought by the slice.

Other shop owners realized the hesitation for holiday shopping and advertised gifts in a wide range of prices. A ring could be bought for as little as a quarter or one could spend as much as $40 on a violin. But even though there may have been consumer apprehension, Christmas was a time that one could justify luxury spending.

In 1843, emphasis was placed on giving to the less fortunate as the classic *A Christmas Carol* emerged. While gifts given to family members during this time were luxurious and presented in person, gifts given to the needy were primarily items of necessity distributed through a charitable organization.

During the Civil War, patriotic gifts were commonly found.

PEACE ON EARTH GOOD WILL TO MEN

For children, toy drums, uniforms, and toy firearms were popular at Christmas and were quickly put to use when the children were play acting. Other typical gifts available were cloth spelling books, toy soldiers, and dolls dressed in patriotic clothing.

After the Civil War, gift-giving in America boomed. Toy stores sprouted up everywhere and more elaborate toys were born. Wind-up

A MERRY CHRISTMAS.

trains, music boxes, Victorian doll houses, and wheeled pull-toys were some of the popular toys that were admired and wished for at Christmastime by boys and girls.

The Victorian approach to gift-giving and gift-making drew the entire family together in celebration. Weeks before Christmas, the family would search the house for bits of scraps from which to make gifts. Drawers flew open and closets were cleaned in hopes of finding fabric pieces, lace remnants, feathers, and more.

From these findings, Christmas gifts were made. Crocheted doilies and cozy warm throws, embroidered slippers and tobacco pouches were just some of the loving gifts Victorians created for one another. Whatever scraps were leftover were carefully turned into elegant ornaments for the tree.

While women of the late 1800s also enjoyed purchased luxury items such as china and jewelry, men wished for practical gifts. A favorite during this time period was the handkerchief. If the relationship was a loving one, a woman would often hand-embroider the handkerchief using strands of her own hair. Souvenirs from famous places or people were also appreciated by men.

With the early 1900s arrived the electric train, beloved teddy bears, matchbox-size cars, and dolls that mirrored celebrities. Today, similar toys bring delight to anxious young ones on Christmas morn.

As Christmases came and went, gifts became more expensive and ornate, each year seeing a new type of sought-after gift. Thousands of holiday items are now available on the commercial market. Today, battery-operated, electronic, and computer-run games and toys are on many a holiday wish list.

Though Christmas gifts and gift-giving have changed from year to year, we continue to celebrate the season of giving just as the Three Wise Men did so long ago as they brought gifts to a tiny baby lying in a manger.

a STAR
in the east

Many years ago in Bethlehem, a star in the East
led the Wise Men to the Baby Jesus. Today, we
celebrate that blessed eve and that perfect star. In
this chapter you'll find a glorious collection of
projects paying tribute to the shining ray of light
that led the way to the most blessed gift of all.

star
PENNY
rug

During the 19th century, scraps of colored felt were often transformed into penny rugs. We've created a colorful holiday version of this vintage craft and featured a star motif in the center. Instructions are on page 84.

Design: Karen Taylor

bethlehem
STAR

Crocheted to resemble the star in the sky so many years ago, our beautiful version is made from white cotton thread. We have stiffened the star so it will hang as the star attraction or to adorn your tree. Instructions are on pages 84–85.

Design: Karen Taylor

<h1>starry night
ORNAMENTS</h1>

Simple red ornaments take on a new light by adding a star motif made from bakeable clay. The stars are uniformly made using aspic cutters and are baked right on the purchased ball. Instructions are on page 85.

Design: Karen Taylor

bright STARS

Simple and whimsical, these happy stars are made using colored pieces of felt and pearl cotton. The pieces are cut and then stuffed for a 3-dimensional effect. Instructions are on pages 85–86.

Design: Phyllis Dunstan

cozy star
QUILT

Cuddle up for the night and watch the stars with your cozy star quilt and matching pillow. These imperfectly shaped stars are all pieced using scraps of printed and plain fabrics. Instructions and patterns are on pages 86–87.

Design: Margaret Sindelar

Design: Margaret Sindelar

shimmering button
ORNAMENTS

Shiny pearl and metallic buttons combine to make beautiful star ornaments.
The buttons are sewn onto a backing and then embellished with tassels and gold
cords. Instructions are on page 88.

Star Penny Rug

As shown on page 78, finished rug is 19 inches in diameter.

MATERIALS
Tracing paper
½ yard of 45-inch-wide green felt
½ yard of 45-inch-wide red felt
12x18-inch piece of white felt
Red and white cotton embroidery floss
Tapestry needle
Fabric glue

INSTRUCTIONS
Trace patterns, *above right*, onto tracing paper; cut out. Cut star from white felt. Also from white, cut thirteen 2½-inch-diameter circles and seven 1½-inch-diameter circles. From red felt, cut 34 pieces using dome-shaped pattern, and seven 2½-inch-diameter circles and thirteen 1½-inch-diameter circles. Cut two 14-inch-diameter circles from green felt.

Work blanket stitches, *page 40*, around star and each circle, using a 6-ply strand of white floss on red and 6-ply strand of red floss on white. Layer two dome-shaped pieces and stitch together using white blanket stitches around curved edge. Repeat for 17 pieces.

Referring to photograph, *page 78*, for placement, glue the star to the center of one green circle. Glue small white circles to centers of large red circles; glue to green felt in circle around star. Glue small red circles to large white circles; glue to green felt around previous circle. Allow glue to dry.

Turn decorated green circle wrong side up. Glue dome-shaped pieces around perimeter, positioning each end 1 inch in toward center and allowing remainder of each piece to extend beyond circle. Glue remaining green circle on top, covering ends of pieces. Turn over; press with hands to secure glued pieces. Allow to dry thoroughly.

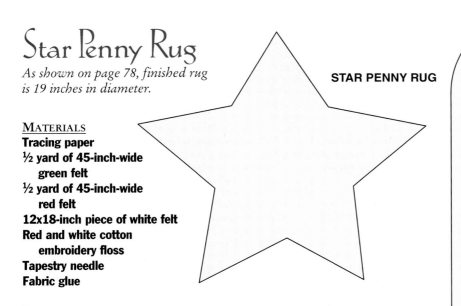

STAR PENNY RUG

Bethlehem Star

As shown on page 79.

MATERIALS
1 ball of white J & P Coats Knit-Cro-Sheen
Size 5 or 6 steel crochet hook
Crafts glue *or* fabric stiffener; T-pins
Plastic kitchen wrap; piece of cardboard

INSTRUCTIONS
Rnd 1: Ch 6; join with sl st to form a ring. Ch 1, work 12 sc in ring; join with sl st in first sc.

Rnd 2: Ch 4 (counts as dc, ch 1), dc in next sc; * ch 1, dc in next dc; rep from * around, ending ch 1; join with sl st in third ch of beginning ch-4. 12 dc.

Rnd 3: Ch 7 (counts as tr, ch 3), tr in next dc; * ch 3, tr in next dc; rep from * around, ending ch 3, join with sl st in fourth ch of beginning ch-7. 12 ch-3 sps.

Rnd 4: In first ch-3 sp [sl st, ch 3 (counts as dc)], 5 dc in same sp; 6 dc in each ch-3 sp around; join with sl st in third ch of beginning ch-3. 72 sts.

Rnd 5: For first point—sc in next st, hdc in next st, 2 dc in next st, in next st (tr, ch 5, tr), 2 dc in next st, hdc in next st, sc in next st, sl st in next 2 sts; for second point—sc in next st, hdc in next st, 2 dc in next st, in next st (tr, ch 2, tr), 2 dc in next st, hdc in next st, sc in next st, sl st in next 2 sts; for third point—

cont as est working (tr, ch 6, tr); for fourth point—work as for second point; for fifth point—work as for first point; for sixth point—work as second point; for seventh point—cont as est working (tr, ch 7, tr); for eighth point—sc in next st, hdc in next st, 2 dc in next st, in next st (tr, ch 2, tr), 2 dc in next st, hdc in next st, sc in next st, sl st in next st.

Rnd 6: Sl st in sl st and next sc, sc in hdc, hdc in dc, dc in dc, dc in tr, in sp (3 tr, ch 3, 3 tr), dc in tr, dc in dc, hdc in dc, sc in hdc, sl st in each of next 4 sts, sc in each of next 4 sts, in sp (3 sc, ch 1, 3 sc), sc in each of next 4 sts, sl st in each of next 4 sts, sc in next st, hdc in next st, dc in each of next 2 sts, in sp (3 tr, ch 4, 3 tr), dc in each of next 2 sts, hdc in next st, sc in next st, sl st in each of next 4 sts, sc in each of next 4 sts, in sp (3 sc, ch 1, 3 sc), sc in each of next 4 sts, sl st in each of next 4 sts, sc in next st, hdc in next st, dc in each of next 2 sts, in sp (3 tr, ch 3, 3 tr), dc in each of next 2 sts, hdc in next st, sc in next st, sl st in each of next 4 sts, sc in each of next 4 sts, in sp (3 sc, ch 1, 3 sc), sc in each of next 4 sts, sl st in each of next 4 sts, sc in next st, hdc in next st, dc in each of next 2 sts, in sp (3 tr, ch 6, 3 tr), dc in each of next 2 sts, hdc in next st, sc in next st, sl st in each of next 4 sts, sc in each of next 4 sts, in sp (3 sc, ch 1, 3 sc), sc in each of next

4 sts, sl st in each of next 2 sts; join with sl st in first sl st and fasten off.

Finishing: Dilute glue slightly with water or follow directions on stiffener. Dip star until saturated with glue mixture. Squeeze out excess. Cover cardboard with plastic wrap and secure with tape on back. Shape star on plastic wrap using T-pins to hold crochet, pulling out points and keeping spacing even. Allow to dry, remove pins, and gently pull plastic wrap away from star. Thread a piece of crochet thread through top point as a hanger.

Starry Night Ornaments

As shown on page 80.

MATERIALS
White bakeable clay; wax paper
Cardboard; rolling pin; crafts knife
½-inch-diameter aspic star
   cookie cutter
Red matte finish glass Christmas
   ball ornaments; small jar lids
Multi-purpose cement (optional)

INSTRUCTIONS
Wash and dry hands. Knead clay with hands until it is soft and pliable.

For Stars ornament, roll clay to a ¹⁄₁₆ inch thickness between sheets of waxed paper. Using cookie cutter, cut out 10 to 13 stars for each ornament. Press stars to ornament at random, spacing evenly. Roll several ⅛-inch-diameter balls from clay; place between stars.

For Noel ornament, roll clay into ⅛-inch-diameter log. Referring to photograph, *page 80,* press pieces of log onto ornament to make 1-inch-tall letters spelling NOEL. Repeat on opposite side. Make stars as for Stars ornament, above; press stars onto ball at random.

Position each ball upright in a jar lid on a cookie sheet. Bake at 275° for 15 minutes. Cool and remove carefully. If the pieces fall off, secure using multi-purpose cement.

Bright Stars

As shown on page 81, stars measure 12×12 inches and 9½×9½ inches.

MATERIALS
Tracing paper; lightweight cardboard
9x12-inch felt rectangles in desired
   colors, three different colors for
   each star
Thread to match felt; pins
Pearl cotton in contrasting color
Large-eyed needle

INSTRUCTIONS
Trace patterns, *below* and *page 86,* onto tracing paper. Cut patterns from cardboard. *Note: Patterns are given for both large and small stars.*

For each large or small star, draw around pattern pieces B and C twice, and piece A and center section once, onto doubled thickness of felt. Cut out pieces. Stitch layers of each point together, leaving bottom short sides unstitched. Use ¼-inch seam allowance for each large star section and ⅛-inch seam allowance for each small star section. Sew center section layers together in same manner, leaving one side unstitched. Do not turn pieces inside out. Stuff each stitched piece lightly and sew across opening to close.

Arrange points around center section for each star, referring to diagram, *below.* Certain size points will only fit against certain sides of center. Overlap seam edge of center section over seam edge of each point; pin in place.

Thread needle with doubled strand of pearl cotton. Sew down through first bottom corner of point, through corresponding corner of center section and back up through the corners to the top. Remove needle, and tie tails in knot to secure. After working all the way around, each corner will be tacked twice. Trim pearl cotton tails to 1 inch.

Thread 8 inches of pearl cotton through top of one point for hanging loop; knot ends.

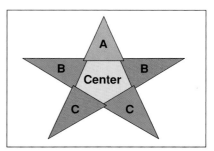

BRIGHT STARS PLACEMENT DIAGRAM

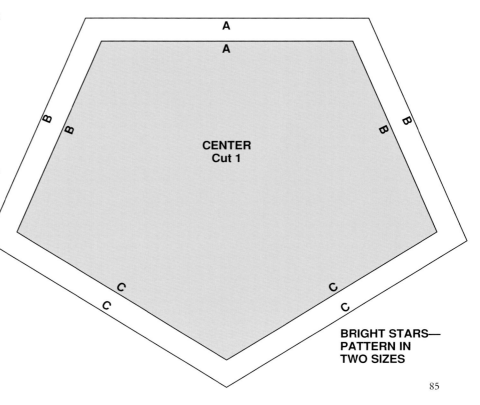

BRIGHT STARS— PATTERN IN TWO SIZES

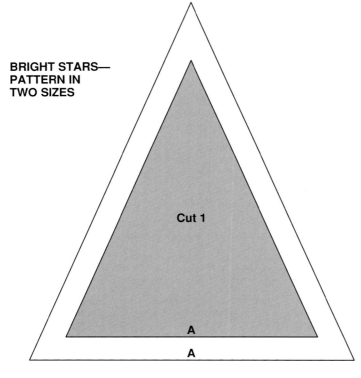

**BRIGHT STARS—
PATTERN IN
TWO SIZES**

Cut 1

A

A

C

C

Cut 2

Cut 2

B

B

Cozy Star Quilt

As shown on page 82, finished size is 58½×65½ inches.

MATERIALS

Fabric yardages are for 45-inch-wide fabrics unless otherwise indicated.
Tracing paper
Quilters' template material
¼ yard *each* of 12 different plaid fabrics
¼ yard *each* of 12 different coordinating solid fabrics
1¼ yard of lavender-gray fabric
1¼ yards of red plaid fabric
2¼ yards of red solid fabric
2¼ yards of 60-inch-wide backing fabric
Clear nylon sewing thread
Polyester batting; eighty 1-inch buttons in assorted colors
Threads to match buttons

INSTRUCTIONS

Enlarge and trace pattern pieces, *page 87.* Cut apart on solid lines. Draw around pieces on template material adding ¼-inch seam allowances. From each of 12 plaid fabrics, cut pieces A, B, C, D, E, and F, turning grainline of plaid at random. From each of 12 solid fabrics, cut pieces 1, 2, 3, 4, and 5.

For sashing, cut sixteen 3½×10½-inch lavender vertical strips, fifteen 3½×12½-inch lavender horizontal strips, and twenty 3½×3½-inch squares from assorted solids.

For border, cut two 4½×70-inch strips and two 4½×62-inch strips from the solid red fabric. Cut red plaid into 3-inch-wide bias binding strips. All measurements include ¼-inch seam allowances. Sew seams with right sides of fabric facing.

For each block, referring to diagram, *below*, sew background pieces 1 and 2 to A. Sew 4 and 5 to D, 3 to B, and C and E to F. Next, stitch piece B3 to piece EFC. To finish, sew three sections of block together.

Arrange blocks in four rows of three blocks each. For each row, sew long side of one vertical sashing strip to each side of left hand block. Sew second block to right sashing. Continuing to work from left to right, sew another sashing, third block, and another sashing.

For horizontal sashing, sew desired color square to each short end of one sashing strip, then sew another sashing strip to the right side of the right-hand square. Continuing to work from left to right, sew a third square, another sashing, and a fourth square. Make five. Sew horizontal sashing between the rows of blocks and at the top and the bottom, matching the seam lines. Sew a red border strip to each side, mitering the corners. Layer quilt top, batting,

and backing (pieced as necessary). Baste. Machine quilt along seam lines of sashing.

Trim the batting and back ½ inch beyond quilt top. Sew enough 3-inch-wide binding strips together to fit around edge of quilt. Pin binding to quilt top, right sides together; stitch through all layers using ¼-inch seam. Miter corners. Turn binding to back of quilt and turn under ¼ inch along raw edge. Slipstitch in place.

Add buttons to corners of each sashing square.

Stars and Buttons Pillow

As shown on page 82, finished size is 20×23 inches.

MATERIALS
Fabric yardages are for 45-inch-wide fabrics unless otherwise indicated.
Tracing paper
Quilters' template material
1½ yards of desired plaid fabric for back and ruffle
¼ yard of desired plaid fabric for star
¼ yard of coordinating solid fabric
¼ yard of blue-gray fabric
Four 3½x3½-inch squares of assorted solid fabrics
Clear nylon sewing thread
Narrow piping cord; polyester fiberfill
Sixteen 1-inch buttons in assorted colors
Threads to match buttons

INSTRUCTIONS
Enlarge and trace pattern and make templates as for Cozy Star Quilt. Cut pieces A, B, C, D, E, and F, from star plaid, and pieces 1, 2, 3, 4, and 5 from solid. Cut two 3½×10½-inch vertical sashing strips and two 3½×12½-inch horizontal sashing strips from blue-gray. Complete a star block as for quilt, *above left,* surrounded by sashing strips.

For ruffle, cut enough 7½-inch-wide plaid strips to measure 4 yards. Sew short ends together to make a circle. Press ruffle in half lengthwise with wrong sides facing.

Position piping cord inside ruffle along folded edge; stitch close to piping using zipper foot. Sew a gathering thread through both layers of ruffle close to raw edges. Pin ruffle to pillow; adjust gathers evenly. Baste ruffle in place.

Use pillow top as pattern to cut plaid pillow back. Sew pillow front to back, right sides facing, using ½-inch seam allowance. Leave opening for turning. Trim seams and clip corners. Turn pillow right side out and stuff with fiberfill. Slipstitch opening closed.

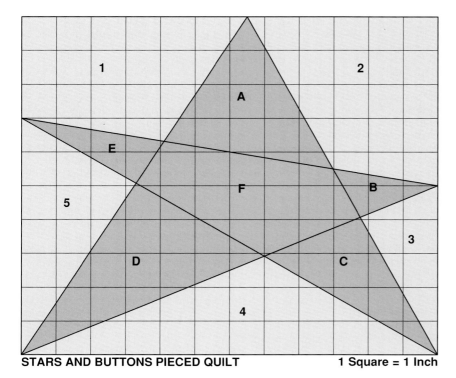

STARS AND BUTTONS PIECED QUILT   **1 Square = 1 Inch**

Shimmering Button Ornaments

As shown on page 83, ornaments measure 4×4 inches and 4½×4½ inches.

MATERIALS

Silver and gold metallic perforated paper
Card stock
Silver and gold metallic wrapping paper
Thick crafts glue
Tracing paper
Silver and gold metallic thread
Tapestry needle
20 to 60 assorted gold, silver, clear, or pearl buttons for each ornament
Silver or gold metallic or beaded tassels (optional)
Silver and gold cord

INSTRUCTIONS

Glue perforated paper to the card stock and then to the wrong side of matching wrapping paper. Trace the star patterns, *right*, onto tracing paper and cut out. Cut the stars as desired from layered papers.

Sew buttons onto the perforated paper side of stars to cover, using matching thread.

Cut 24 inches of matching cord for hanging loop. Tack the center of the cord to the back of the star at the top point. Knot the ends. Tack the tassel to the bottom of the star. If desired, glue another layer of wrapping paper to the back of the star to cover the threads; trim to match the shape.

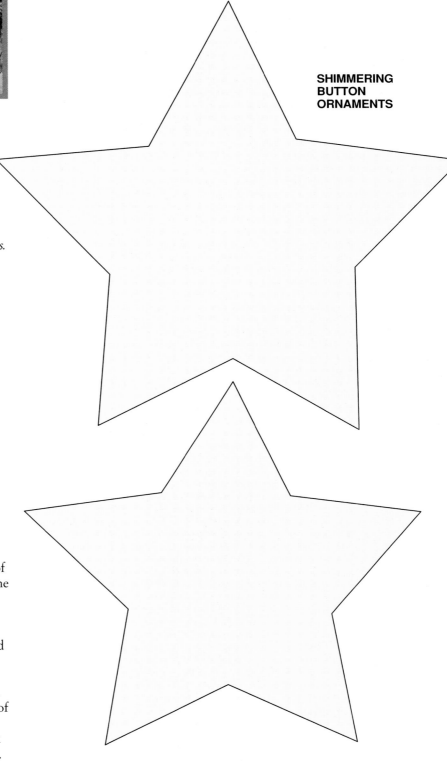

SHIMMERING BUTTON ORNAMENTS

happy HOLIDAY celebrations

Gathering together with family and friends at Christmastime is just one of the grand pleasures of the holiday season. Young and old alike look forward to those special occasions when food and fun combine, creating lasting memories. In this chapter we've planned some gala celebrations for you to share with the ones you love.

COOKIE EXCHANGE

Invite only famous (or infamous) cookie lovers into your kitchen—all bearing cookies most dear to their hearts. They'll arrive with old family favorites and leave carrying fresh ones, smitten with cookie possibilities. Turn the page for clever cookie container ideas and recipes for all the cookies you see here.

COOKIE
containers

Razzle, dazzle containers are the fitting final step for your tasty treasures. Give your guests packaging options that will bowl them over. See ideas and tips for creating your own clever containers on the next page.

White Chocolate Cherry Twists

As shown on pages 90–91.

INGREDIENTS

- 3/4 cup butter, softened
- 1 cup sugar
- 1 teaspoon baking powder
- 1 egg
- 1 teaspoon vanilla
- 2 1/2 cups all-purpose flour
- 1/3 cup finely chopped candied red cherries
- Few drops red food coloring
- 2 ounces white chocolate baking squares, finely chopped
- 2 ounces white chocolate baking squares, chopped, optional
- 2 teaspoons shortening, optional

METHOD

In a large mixing bowl beat the butter with an electric mixer on medium to high speed about 30 seconds or till softened. Add the sugar and baking powder; beat till combined. Beat in the egg and vanilla. Beat in as much of the flour as you can with the mixer. Using a wooden spoon, stir in any remaining flour. Divide dough.

To half of the dough stir in the chopped candied cherries and food coloring till combined. To the remaining half of the dough stir in 2 ounces finely chopped white chocolate. Wrap each portion of dough in clear plastic wrap or waxed paper and chill for 30 minutes or till dough is easy to handle.

For each cookie, on a lightly floured surface, shape a slightly rounded teaspoonful of red dough into a 6-inch rope. Repeat with a teaspoonful of white chocolate dough. Place ropes side by side and twist together. Pinch ends to seal. Form twisted ropes into canes, if desired. Place twists or canes 2 inches apart on an ungreased cookie sheet. Bake cookies in a 375° oven for 8 to 10 minutes or till edges are firm and light brown. Cool cookies on cookie sheet for 1 minute. Remove cookies from cookie sheet and cool on a wire rack.

If desired, in a heavy small saucepan melt the 2 ounces white chocolate baking squares and the 2 teaspoons shortening over very low heat till chocolate melts, stirring constantly. Drizzle mixture over cookies. Let stand till chocolate sets. Place cookies in a single layer in an airtight container and store at room temperature for up to 3 days. Makes 56 cookies.

Sugar Cookie Dough

Used for Cashew Cookies and Frosted Sugar Cookie Cutouts recipes, page 94, and Chocolate Mint Pillows recipe, page 97.

INGREDIENTS

- 3/4 cup butter
- 3/4 cup shortening
- 2 cups sugar
- 2 teaspoons baking powder
- 1/2 teaspoon salt
- 4 eggs
- 2 teaspoons vanilla
- 5 cups all-purpose flour

METHOD

In a large mixing bowl beat together the butter and shortening with an electric mixer on medium to high speed about 30 seconds or till combined. Add the sugar, baking powder, and salt. Beat till combined, scraping bowl. Beat in the eggs and vanilla. Beat in as much of the flour as you can with the mixer. Stir in any remaining flour.

Divide dough into 3 portions. If necessary, cover and chill dough for 3 hours or till easy to handle. Use dough to make Cashew Cookies, Frosted Sugar Cookie Cutouts, and Chocolate-Mint Pillows.

Cashew Cookies

As shown on pages 90–91.

INGREDIENTS
- 1/3 recipe Sugar Cookie Dough (see *page 93*)
- 1/2 cup finely chopped cashews
- 1 slightly beaten egg white
- 1 cup finely chopped cashews
- 36 whole cashews

METHOD
In a medium mixing bowl combine the 1/3 recipe cookie dough and 1/2 cup finely chopped cashews. Using a wooden spoon, stir till combined. Wrap dough in clear plastic wrap or waxed paper and chill about 3 hours or till dough is easy to handle.

Lightly grease 2 cookie sheets. Shape dough into 1-inch balls. Roll in egg white, then in the 1 cup finely chopped cashews. Place balls 2 inches apart on the prepared cookie sheets. Using the bottom of a glass or your hand, slightly flatten each cookie. Carefully press a whole cashew onto the top of each cookie. Bake in a 350° oven for 8 to 10 minutes or till cookies are just lightly browned on bottom. Carefully remove cookies from cookie sheet and cool on a wire rack. Makes 36 cookies.

Frosted Sugar Cookie Cutouts

As shown on pages 90–91.

INGREDIENTS
- 1/3 recipe Sugar Cookie Dough (see *page 93*)
- 1 recipe Meringue Powder Glaze (see *right*) or other desired icing, optional

METHOD
On a well-floured surface, roll one half of dough (keeping remaining dough chilled) to 1/4-inch thickness. Using desired cookie cutters and dipping into flour between cuts, cut dough into shapes. Place cookies 1 inch apart on an ungreased cookie sheet. Bake in a 375° oven for 6 to 8 minutes or till edges are firm and bottoms are very lightly browned. Cool cookies on cookie sheet for 1 minute. Carefully remove from cookie sheet and cool on a wire rack. Decorate cookies as desired. Makes about 36 cookies.

Meringue Powder Glaze:
In a medium mixing bowl beat together 2 tablespoons meringue powder, 1/4 cup warm water, and 2 cups sifted powdered sugar with a fork till smooth. Gradually stir in about 1½ cups additional sifted powdered sugar to make a smooth glaze that is spreadable but not runny. (It should have a flowing consistency and be too thin to hold ridges when spread.) Using powdered or liquid food coloring, color glaze as desired.

To Make Ahead:
Bake cookies as directed, except *do not* frost. Place cooled cookies in a freezer container and freeze for up to 1 month. Before serving, let cookies thaw. Decorate as desired.

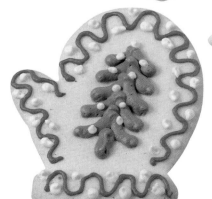

Whimsical Gingerbread Cookies

Shown on pages 90–91.

INGREDIENTS

- 1 cup butter
- 2/3 cup packed brown sugar
- 2/3 cup molasses
- 4 cups all-purpose flour
- 2 teaspoons finely shredded orange peel
- 1 1/3 teaspoons ground cinnamon
- 1 teaspoon ground ginger
- 3/4 teaspoon baking soda
- 1/4 teaspoon ground cloves
- 1 egg
- 1 1/3 teaspoons vanilla
- 1 recipe Butter Frosting (see *right*)

METHOD

In a medium saucepan combine the butter, brown sugar, and molasses. Stir over medium heat just till butter melts and sugar dissolves. Pour into a large mixing bowl; cool for 5 minutes.

Meanwhile, in another bowl stir together the flour, orange peel, cinnamon, ginger, baking soda, and cloves; set aside.

Add the egg and vanilla to butter mixture; mix well. Add the flour mixture and beat at low speed till well combined. (If necessary, stir in last portion of flour mixture by hand.) Divide dough in half. Wrap each dough portion in clear plastic wrap or waxed paper and chill at least 2 hours or overnight.

Shape cookies as directed, *right.* Bake in a 350° oven for 8 to 10 minutes or till edges are firm. Cool on the cookie sheet for 1 minute. Using a wide metal spatula, carefully remove cookies from cookie sheets and cool on a wire rack. Decorate as desired using Butter Frosting, *right,* to pipe onto cooled cookies, adding expressions and details such as eyes, mouths, etc., and to add some color to the cookies such as the hat on the snowman or decorations on the trees. Makes about 24 to 30 cookies (varies with shape selected).

For each reindeer, shape dough into one 1 1/4-inch ball and three 1/2-inch balls. On an ungreased cookie sheet flatten the 1 1/4-inch ball to 1/2-inch and form it into a diamond shape for the head. Flatten one of the 1/2-inch balls to 1/2-inch to form the nose; place it on top of the head, slightly lower than center. Shape the remaining 1/2-inch balls into long diamonds and attach to the head for ears. Use broken pretzel twists for antlers, inserting into dough at top of head.

For each snowman, shape dough into one 1-inch ball, one 3/4-inch ball, two 1/2-inch balls, and one 1/4-inch ball. On an ungreased cookie sheet flatten the 1-inch ball to 1/2-inch for the body. Flatten the 3/4-inch ball to 1/2-inch and attach to the body for the head. Shape one of the 1/2-inch balls into a triangle and attach to the head for a hat. Shape the other 1/2-inch ball into a log about 1-inch long; place it between the hat and the head, atop the dough, curving to fit like a brim. Attach the 1/4-inch ball at the tip of the hat to form a tassel. If desired, shape another 1/4-inch ball into a ball and place on head for the nose. Insert broken pretzel twists for arms, if desired.

For each tree, shape dough into one 1-inch ball, one 3/4-inch ball, one 1/2-inch ball, and one 1/4-inch ball. On an ungreased cookie sheet flatten the 1-inch ball to 1/2-inch and shape it into a triangle. Flatten the 3/4-inch ball to 1/2-inch; shape it into a triangle, and attach it to the peak of the large triangle, slightly overlapping. Shape the 1/2-inch ball into a triangle and attach it to the second triangle, slightly overlapping at the point. Attach the 1/4-inch ball to the middle of the bottom triangle for a trunk. If desired, shape another 1/4-inch ball into a star and place atop the tree.

Butter Frosting:

In mixing bowl combine 1/3 cup melted butter, 3 cups sifted powdered sugar, and enough milk (about 2 to 3 tbsp.) to make of piping consistency. Tint frosting using liquid or paste food coloring as desired.

To Make Ahead:

Bake cookies as directed, except *do not* decorate with frosting. Place the cooled cookies in a single layer in a freezer container and freeze for up to 1 month. Before serving, let thaw. Decorate as desired.

Anise Hazelnut Tea Cakes

As shown on pages 90–91.

INGREDIENTS

1	cup butter
2¼	cups all-purpose flour
½	cup sifted powdered sugar
1	tablespoon water
1	teaspoon anise seed, crushed
1	teaspoon vanilla
¾	cup finely chopped hazelnuts (filberts), almonds, or pecans
1	cup sifted powdered sugar
½	teaspoon powdered food coloring (optional)

METHOD

In a large mixing bowl beat the butter with an electric mixer on medium to high speed for 30 seconds. Add half of the flour; beat at low speed till combined. Add the ½ cup powdered sugar, water, anise seed, and vanilla. Beat just till combined. Beat or stir in remaining flour. Stir in nuts. Cover and chill dough about 1 hour or till easy to handle.

Shape dough into 1-inch balls. Place cookies 1-inch apart on an ungreased cookie sheet. Bake in a 325° oven for 18 to 20 minutes or till bottoms are lightly browned. Remove cookies from cookie sheet and cool on a wire rack.

In a self-sealing plastic bag place the 1 cup powdered sugar and, if desired, the powdered food coloring. Add a few cookies to the bag at a time and shake gently to coat. Place cookies in an airtight container and store at room temperature up to 3 days. Makes about 4½ dozen cookies. *(Note: If powdered food coloring is omitted, coat cookies again with additional powdered sugar just before serving.)*

To Make Ahead:

Bake cookies as directed, except *do not* toss with the powdered sugar before freezing. Place cooled cookies in a freezer bag or container and freeze for up to 1 month. Before serving, let cookies thaw. Toss with powdered sugar mixture before serving.

Cranberry Apricot Florentines

As shown on pages 90–91.

INGREDIENTS

⅓	cup butter or margarine
⅓	cup milk
¼	cup sugar
1	cup finely chopped macadamia nuts or sliced almonds
½	cup snipped dried cranberries or dried tart red cherries
¼	cup snipped dried apricots
¼	cup all-purpose flour
¾	cup semisweet chocolate pieces
2	teaspoons shortening
2	ounces white chocolate baking squares, chopped
2	teaspoons shortening

METHOD

Grease and flour a cookie sheet. (Repeat greasing and flouring cookie sheet for each batch.) Set aside.

In a heavy medium saucepan combine the butter or margarine, milk, and sugar. Bring to a full rolling boil, stirring occasionally. Remove from heat. Stir in the macadamia nuts or almonds, cranberries or cherries, and apricots. Stir in the flour.

Drop the batter from a level tablespoon at least 3 inches apart onto the prepared cookie sheet. Using the back of a spoon, spread batter into 3-inch circles.

Bake in a 350° oven about 8 minutes or till edges are lightly browned. Cool on the cookie sheet for 1 minute. Carefully remove cookies from cookie sheet and cool on waxed paper.

In a heavy small saucepan heat the semisweet chocolate pieces and 2 teaspoons shortening over very low heat just till melted, stirring occasionally. In another heavy small saucepan heat the white chocolate and 2 teaspoons shortening over very low heat just till melted, stirring occasionally.

Spread the bottom of each cookie with a scant teaspoon of the semisweet chocolate mixture. Drizzle the white chocolate mixture onto the dark chocolate. To marble, draw the tines of a fork through the white chocolate. Let cookies stand, chocolate side up, till chocolate is set. Place cookies in a single layer in an airtight container and store in the refrigerator for up to 3 days. Makes about 24.

Lemon Poppy Seed Shortbread

Shown on pages 90–91.

INGREDIENTS

2 1/3 **cups all-purpose flour**
  1/3 **cup sugar**
   1 **tablespoon poppy seed**
   1 **cup butter**
   2 **teaspoons finely shredded lemon peel**
   1 **recipe Lemon Glaze (see *right*)**
    Coarse pastel multi-colored sugar

METHOD

In a large mixing bowl stir together the flour, sugar, and poppy seed. Using a pastry blender, cut in the butter till mixture resembles fine crumbs and starts to cling. Stir in the lemon peel. Form the mixture into a ball and knead till smooth.

On a lightly floured surface, roll dough to slightly less than ½-inch thickness. Using 1½ to 2 inch cookie cutters, cut dough into shapes. Place the cookies 1 inch apart on an ungreased cookie sheet. Bake in a 325° oven for 20 to 25 minutes or till bottoms start to just turn brown. Remove cookies from cookie sheet and cool on a wire rack.

Lightly spread cookies with Lemon Glaze. Sprinkle with multi-colored sugar. Let cookies stand till glaze is set. Place in an airtight container and store at room temperature up to 3 days. Makes about 16 to 20 cookies.

Lemon Glaze:
In a small bowl stir together 1½ cups sifted powdered sugar, 2 teaspoons lemon juice, and enough milk (about 2 tablespoons) to make glaze easy to spread.

To Make Ahead:
Bake cookies as directed, except *do not* glaze. Place cooled cookies in a freezer bag or container and freeze for up to 1 month. Before serving, thaw cookies for 15 minutes. Glaze and sprinkle with sugar as directed.

Chocolate Mint Pillows

Shown on pages 90–91.

INGREDIENTS

  1/3 **recipe Sugar Cookie Dough (see *page 93*)**
  1/4 **teaspoon mint extract**
    Few drops green food coloring
   4 **1.55-ounce bars milk chocolate**

METHOD

In a medium mixing bowl combine the ⅓ recipe cookie dough, the mint extract, and green food coloring. Using a wooden spoon, stir till combined and dough is a light to medium green. If necessary, add more coloring. Divide the dough in half. Wrap each half in clear plastic wrap or waxed paper and chill about 3 hours or till dough is easy to handle.

On a lightly floured surface, roll one portion of dough (keeping other portion chilled) into a 10×6-inch rectangle. Cut into fifteen 2-inch squares. Break

chocolate bars into rectangles along markings. Place one small rectangle of chocolate on one half of each of the squares of dough. Bring other half of dough up and over to cover chocolate and form a rectangle. Place squares 1 inch apart on the prepared cookie sheet. Using a fork, press edges together to seal. Repeat with other portion of dough.

Bake cookies in a 375° oven for 8 to 10 minutes or till edges are firm and bottoms are lightly browned. Remove cookies from cookie sheet and cool on a wire rack.

Place remaining pieces of chocolate in a heavy small saucepan and heat over very low heat just till melted, stirring almost constantly. Spoon melted chocolate into a small self-sealing plastic bag. Seal bag and snip a small corner from bag. Pipe a small scroll or other design onto tops of cooled cookies. Place cookies in refrigerator for a few minutes till chocolate is set. Place cookies in a single layer in an airtight container and store at room temperature for up to 3 days. Makes 30 cookies.

IT'S A WRAP BUFFET

In the midst of all the holiday hoopla, take a deep breath and concentrate on the reason for the season. To celebrate this time of giving, give a party where everyone can wrap gifts for charity or a favorite cause. Party paper and decorations can work double duty as gift wrap and trims needed for packages. Then, surprise your guests by serving a generous buffet to celebrate friendship and the season of giving. All the recipes for the goodies you see here start on page 106.

wraps and
RIBBONS
centerpiece

A colorful bouquet of wrapping papers planted in a crystal bowl is a centerpiece that works. Instead of full rolls of paper, cut the paper into manageable pieces and reroll them using bright curling ribbon. Scissors with bright handles stand tall in a crystal vase and a glass candy dish holds clear tape. Colorful bowls hold yards of shiny ribbons with pens and gift tags.

ribbon scrap
WRAPS

Every scrap of ribbon has a special place when you combine them to create a pleasant mixture of color and texture atop your favorite gift papers. Tiny snippets of ribbon form a tiny tree and layers of ribbon combine to make a plain wrap oh-so-fancy.

Design: Carol Dahlstrom

Golden jingle bells sing when tied to the ends of our curling ribbon bow.

Designs: Carol Dahlstrom

Black and white make a happy holiday statement when trimmed with buttons and curling ribbon.

Ponytail holders and ribbons combine for delightful doodad gift toppers!

Dress up a silver doily with a real or candy coin and glue atop a favorite paper.

merry Christmas!

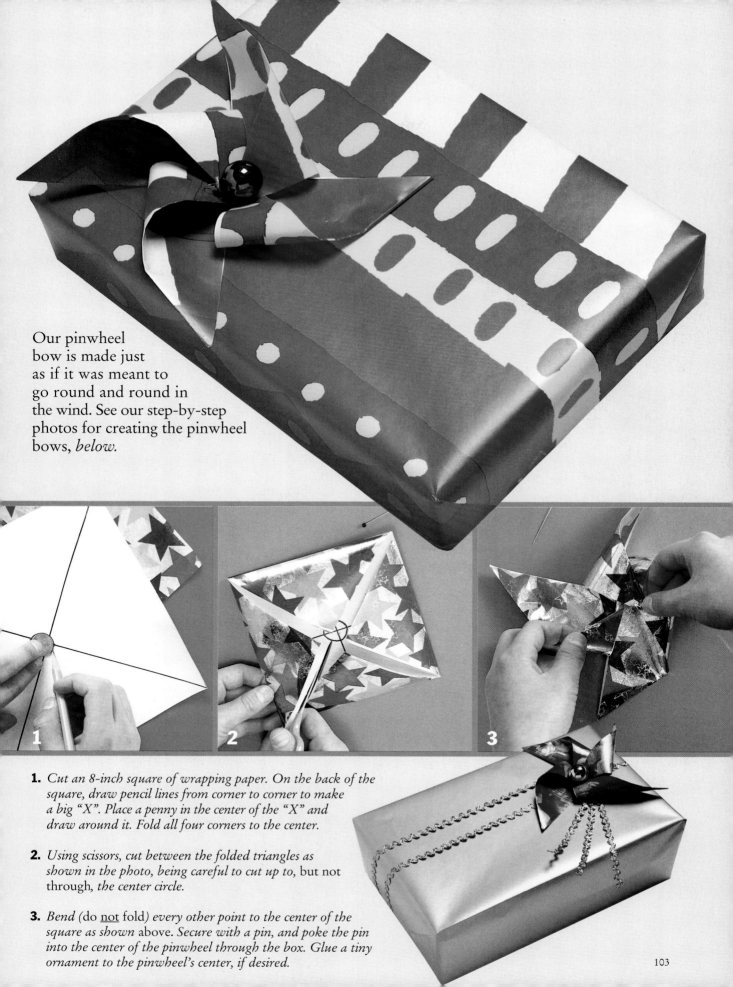

Our pinwheel
bow is made just
as if it was meant to
go round and round in
the wind. See our step-by-step
photos for creating the pinwheel
bows, *below.*

1. *Cut an 8-inch square of wrapping paper. On the back of the
square, draw pencil lines from corner to corner to make
a big "X". Place a penny in the center of the "X" and
draw around it. Fold all four corners to the center.*

2. *Using scissors, cut between the folded triangles as
shown in the photo, being careful to cut up to,* but not
through, *the center circle.*

3. *Bend (do* **not** *fold) every other point to the center of the
square as shown* above. *Secure with a pin, and poke the pin
into the center of the pinwheel through the box. Glue a tiny
ornament to the pinwheel's center, if desired.*

103

sweetly
DECORATED
treats

Candy can play dress-up too! Use pastel candy coating to add swirls of color to sleek Chocolate Covered Cherries. Our Lemon Crunch Candy is quick to make and sure to disappear fast! Recipes for both candies are on page 107.

a wreath of
VEGETABLES

Vegetables combine in a wreath for simple snacking while wrapping gifts.
We've added a shiny ribbon bow to make the wreath seem complete.
Instructions for making this wreath of vegetables are on page 107.

Holiday Meatballs

As shown on pages 98–99.

INGREDIENTS

- 1 beaten egg
- 3/4 cup soft bread crumbs
- 1/4 cup chopped pistachio nuts or almonds
- 1/4 cup chopped cranberries
- 2 tablespoons chopped onion
- 1/4 teaspoon salt
- 1/8 teaspoon ground allspice
- 8 ounces ground pork or ground raw chicken or turkey
- 8 ounces ground pork sausage or turkey sausage
  Nonstick spray coating
- 1 10-ounce jar currant jelly
- 2/3 cup catsup
- 1 tablespoon lemon juice
- 1/2 to 1 teaspoon grated ginger root

METHOD

For meatballs, in a large mixing bowl combine the egg, bread crumbs, pistachio nuts, cranberries, onion, salt, and allspice. Add ground pork, chicken, or turkey and the pork sausage; mix well. Shape into 36 meatballs.

Spray a 15×10×1-inch baking pan with nonstick coating. Place meatballs in pan. Bake in a 350° oven for 15 to 18 minutes or till no longer pink inside.

Meanwhile, for sauce, in a medium saucepan combine the jelly, catsup, lemon juice, and ginger root. Cook and stir over low heat till jelly melts. Add meatballs; heat through. Makes 36.

Note: For small groups, serve half the recipe at a time. The sauce will halve easily.

Chevre and Spinach Phyllo Bundles

As shown on pages 98–99.

INGREDIENTS

- 1/2 of 10-ounce package frozen chopped spinach, thawed and well-drained
- 1/3 cup chopped shallots or sliced green onions
- 1 clove garlic, minced
- 4 ounces soft goat cheese (chevre)
- 1 3-ounce package cream cheese, softened
- 1/3 cup golden raisins
- 1 tablespoon snipped fresh dill or 1/2 teaspoon dried dillweed
- 1/8 teaspoon pepper
- 9 sheets (18x14-inches) frozen phyllo dough, thawed
- 1/3 cup margarine or butter, melted

METHOD

In a medium saucepan cook shallots or green onions and garlic in a small amount of boiling water till tender, about 4 minutes. Drain. Add the spinach, goat cheese, cream cheese, raisins, dill, and pepper to the mixture in the saucepan. Stir till combined.

Unfold phyllo dough. Place 1 sheet of phyllo dough on a work surface, keeping remaining sheets covered with plastic wrap. Generously brush the sheet with some of the melted margarine or butter. Top with another sheet of phyllo, then brush with more of the margarine or butter. Repeat with a third sheet of phyllo and margarine or butter.

Using a sharp knife, cut into eight rectangles, about 7×4½ inches. Place about 1 tablespoon filling in the center of each rectangle. For each bundle, bring 4 corners together; pinch and twist slightly.

Repeat with remaining phyllo dough, margarine or butter, and filling to make 24 bundles total. Arrange bundles on an ungreased baking sheet. Bake, uncovered, in a 375° oven for 10 to 12 minutes or till golden. Serve warm. Makes 24.

To Make Ahead:
Prepare bundles as directed, except *do not* bake. Place unbaked bundles in a single layer on baking sheets and freeze till firm. Place frozen bundles in a freezer container. seal and freeze for up to 3 months.

To serve, place frozen bundles on an ungreased parchment- or foil-lined baking sheet. *Do not* thaw before baking or pastries will be soggy. Bake, uncovered, in a 375° oven about 15 minutes or till golden. Makes 24.

Hot Buttered Berry–Apple Cider

As shown on pages 98–99.

INGREDIENTS

- 7 cups apple cider or apple juice
- 1 10-ounce package frozen red raspberries in syrup
- 2 tablespoons brown sugar
- 4 inches stick cinnamon
- 1 teaspoon whole allspice
- 1 teaspoon whole cloves
  Peel from 1 orange, cut into thin strips
- 1 cup apple brandy or rum
  Butter
  Orange peel curls, thin orange slices, or fresh red raspberries (optional)

METHOD

In a kettle or pot combine the apple cider or juice, raspberries, brown sugar, stick cinnamon, allspice, cloves, and orange peel strips. Bring to boiling. Reduce heat and simmer, covered, for 10 minutes.

Line a sieve with 100-percent-cotton cheesecloth. Strain the mixture through the sieve. Stir the apple brandy or rum into the mixture.

To serve, pour the cider into heat-proof glasses, cups, or mugs. Float ½ teaspoon butter on each.

If desired, garnish each serving with orange peel curls, thin orange slices, or fresh red raspberries. Makes 11 (6-ounce) servings.

Chocolate Covered Cherries

As shown on page 104.

INGREDIENTS
- **60 maraschino cherries with stems**
- **3 tablespoons butter, softened**
- **3 tablespoons light-colored corn syrup**
- **2 cups sifted powdered sugar**
- **1 pound chocolate-flavored candy coating, chopped**
- **2 ounces pastel vanilla-flavored candy coating (optional)**

METHOD
Drain cherries thoroughly on paper towels for several hours. Line a baking sheet with waxed paper; set baking sheet aside.

In a small mixing bowl combine the butter and corn syrup. Stir in powdered sugar. Knead the mixture till smooth (chill if the mixture is too soft to handle). Shape about ½ teaspoon powdered sugar mixture around each cherry. Place coated cherries, stem sides up, on prepared baking sheet; chill about 1 hour or till firm (do not chill too long or sugar mixture will begin to dissolve).

In a heavy medium saucepan melt chocolate-flavored candy coating over low heat, stirring constantly. Holding cherries by stems, dip one at a time into the coating. If necessary, spoon coating over cherries to coat. (Be sure to completely seal cherries in coating to prevent juice from leaking.) Let excess coating drip off. Place cherries, stem sides up, on prepared baking sheet.

Chill till coating is firm. (Check bottoms of cherries to see if well sealed. If necessary spread bottoms with additional melted chocolate to seal.) If desired, in a heavy small saucepan melt the pastel vanilla-flavored candy coating over low heat, stirring constantly. Using

a decorating bag fitted with a small round tip, decorate dipped cherries with dots, stripes, zigzags, swirls, or a combination. Place cherries in a tightly covered container in the refrigerator. Let candies ripen in the refrigerator for 1 to 2 weeks before serving. (Ripening allows powdered sugar mixture around cherries to soften and liquefy.) Bring to room temperature before serving. Makes 60 pieces.

Pastel Colored Candy Coating: Melt additional vanilla flavored candy coating and stir in desired food coloring paste, a little at a time, till desired pastel color is achieved.

Lemon Crunch Candy

As shown on page 104.

INGREDIENTS
- **1 pound vanilla-flavored candy coating, cut up**
- **3/4 cup crushed hard lemon, orange, strawberry, cherry or peppermint candies**

METHOD
Line a baking sheet with foil; set aside. In a heavy medium saucepan melt candy coating over low heat, stirring constantly. Remove saucepan from heat. Stir in crushed candies. Pour melted mixture onto the prepared baking sheet. Spread mixture to about a ⅜-inch thickness.

Chill candy about 30 minutes or till firm. (Or, let candy stand at room

temperature for several hours or till firm.) Use foil to lift firm candy from baking sheet; carefully break candy into pieces. Place in an airtight container and store at room temperature for up to 2 weeks. Makes about 1¼ pounds (20 servings).

Horseradish Dip and Vegetables

As shown on page 105.

INGREDIENTS
- **1 cup regular or light mayonnaise or salad dressing**
- **1/2 cup regular or light dairy sour cream**
- **3 tablespoons snipped fresh chives**
- **1 tablespoon prepared horseradish**
- **1 teaspoon Dijon-style mustard**
- **1 clove garlic, minced**
- **1/8 teaspoon pepper**
  Assorted salad greens
  Assorted vegetables, such as green, red, and/or yellow sweet pepper strips; jicama slices; carrots; and zucchini and/or yellow summer squash

METHOD
In a small mixing bowl stir together the mayonnaise or salad dressing, sour cream, chives, horseradish, Dijon-style mustard, garlic, and pepper. Cover and chill in the refrigerator for 2 to 24 hours. To store, transfer to an airtight container and store in refrigerator for up to 2 days.

To serve, transfer the dip to a small bowl. Place the bowl in the center of a lettuce-lined basket or glass platter. Using cookie cutters in desired shapes, cut the sweet pepper strips and jicama slices into festive shapes. Using a vegetable peeler, cut the carrots and zucchini and/or yellow summer squash into thin ribbons. Arrange the vegetables among the lettuce to resemble a wreath. Makes about 1⅔ cups of dip (28 1-tablespoon servings).

SNOWMAN CELEBRATION

You've built the grandest snowman—so pull up to the table and warm up with some Make-Ahead Minestrone and Tortilla Roll Ups. Big Soft Ginger Cookies and White Hot Chocolate make the day extra cozy. Keep those snowmen coming with a tableful of snowman friends printed on the tablecloth and a sidekick snowman made from a stack of marshmallows. Recipes begin on page 111.

Snowman building is hard work. A cool sparkling punch will quench your thirst as you admire your handmade tablecloth. Recipes and instructions are on page 112.

Design: Carol Dahlstrom

Make-Ahead Minestrone

As shown on pages 108–109.

INGREDIENTS

- 3 14½-ounce cans beef broth
- 2 15-ounce can canellini beans or small white beans, rinsed and drained
- 1 14½-ounce can Italian-style stewed tomatoes
- 1 1½-ounce can vegetable juice
- 1 6-ounce can tomato paste
- 2 teaspoons sugar
- 1 teaspoon dried Italian seasoning, crushed
- 1½ cups loose-pack frozen mixed vegetables (such as an Italian blend)
- 2 cups fresh spinach leaves, cut in strips
- 2 cups cooked pasta (1 cup uncooked), elbow macaroni or snowman pasta
  Finely shredded Parmesan cheese

METHOD

In a large kettle combine broth, beans, stewed tomatoes, vegetable juice, tomato paste, sugar, and Italian seasoning. Bring to boiling. Add mixed vegetables. Reduce heat. Cover and simmer about 10 minutes or until vegetables are tender. Remove from heat; cool slightly. Transfer to large storage container. Refrigerate, covered, overnight. (Or, to serve immediately, add spinach and cooked pasta; heat through.)

To serve, return soup to large kettle and reheat soup over medium heat. Stir in spinach and cooked pasta. Heat through. To serve, ladle into bowls. Sprinkle with Parmesan cheese. Makes 8 main-dish servings.

Tortilla Roll Ups

As shown on pages 108–109.

INGREDIENTS

- 6 8 to 10-inch red and/or green colored flour tortillas
- 1 8-ounce tub cream cheese with garden vegetables (soft-style)
- 1 6-ounce package thinly sliced cooked turkey or ham
- 6 lettuce leaves
- 1 medium red pepper, cut into thin strips or 2 medium carrots, cut into julienne strips

METHOD

Spread one side of each tortilla with 1 well-rounded tablespoon cream cheese. Top with turkey or ham, a lettuce leaf, and some red pepper or carrot strips. Roll up tortillas tightly. May wrap and store in refrigerator up to 24 hours. Serves 6.

White Hot Chocolate

INGREDIENTS

- 3 cups half-and-half or light cream
- ⅔ cup vanilla-flavor baking pieces or vanilla-flavor candy coating, chopped
- 3 inches stick cinnamon
- ½ teaspoon ground nutmeg
- 1 teaspoon vanilla
- ¼ teaspoon almond extract
  Peppermint sticks, optional

METHOD

Combine ¼ cup of the half-and-half or light cream, vanilla-flavor pieces or vanilla-flavor coating, stick cinnamon, and nutmeg in a medium saucepan. Whisk over low heat till vanilla-flavor pieces or coating is melted. Remove stick cinnamon.

Add the remaining half-and-half or cream. Whisk till heated through. Remove from heat. Stir in vanilla and almond extract.

Serve warm in mugs. Garnish with peppermint sticks, if desired. Makes 5 (6-ounce) servings.

Big Soft Ginger Cookies

As shown on pages 108–109.

INGREDIENTS

- 1 cup butter or margarine
- 1 cup sugar
- 2 teaspoons baking soda
- 2 teaspoons grated ginger root (or 1 teaspoon ground ginger)
- 1 teaspoon ground nutmeg
- ½ teaspoon ground cloves
- 2 eggs
- ⅔ cup molasses
- 4 cups all-purpose flour
  Lemon Icing (see recipe *below*)

METHOD

In large mixing bowl beat butter with electric mixer on medium to high speed about 30 seconds or until softened. Add sugar, soda, ginger root, nutmeg, and cloves; beat till combined. Beat in eggs and molasses till combined, scraping sides of bowl occasionally. Beat in as much of the flour as you can with the mixer. Stir in any remaining flour with a wooden spoon.

Drop dough a scant ¼ cup at a time, 3 inches apart, onto ungreased cookie sheet. Bake in 350° oven 12 to 14 minutes or until edges are firm. Cool on the cookie sheet for 1 minute. With a wide metal spatula, remove cookies to a wire rack. Spoon Lemon Icing over warm cookies to glaze tops, or drizzle icing in a zigzag pattern, write names, or draw snowflakes or other designs on the cookies. Makes 22 to 24 cookies.

Lemon Icing:

In small bowl combine 2 cups sifted powdered sugar, 2 tablespoons lemon juice, and enough milk (about 1 to 2 teaspoons) to make an icing of drizzling consistency.

Fizzy Fruit Punch

As shown on page 110.

INGREDIENTS
- 5 cups cranberry-apple drink
- ¼ cup lemon juice
- 3 tablespoons grenadine syrup
- 28 ounces lemon-lime carbonated beverage or club soda
- Ice cubes
- Lime slices or lime peel curls, optional
- Coarsely granulated sugar, optional

METHOD
Stir together cranberry-apple drink, lemon juice, and grenadine in a large pitcher. Slowly pour the lemon-lime carbonated beverage or club soda down the side of the pitcher; stir gently. Serve over ice cubes in wine glasses. Garnish with lime slices or lime peel curls, if desired. Makes 12 (6-ounce) servings.

To make the "snow" on the outside ring of the cup and punch bowl, moisten the rim with water and dip in coarsely granulated sugar before filling with punch.

Friendly Snowman Tablecloth

As shown on page 110.

MATERIALS
Waxed paper
Washable light blue felt fabric in desired size
Fabric Paint: White, black, red, blue, yellow, and orange
Disposable plastic plates
Potatoes in three sizes
Sharp knife
Pencil with new eraser
Old clothespin

INSTRUCTIONS
Cover work surface with waxed paper. Lay the fabric on the covered surface.

Cut the largest potato in half. Spread the white paint on a disposable plate and dip the potato in the paint. Stamp the tablecloth where desired making the bottom of the snowmen.

Cut the next size potato in half. Repeat for centers of snowmen. Repeat using the smallest potato for the heads.

Cut one of the remaining potato halves away leaving the shape of a hat. Print with black paint. Using a pencil eraser, dip the pencil in black for the eyes and bright colors for the buttons. Take the clothespin apart and use the end for the noses and the sides for the arms. Allow to dry.

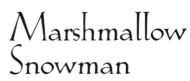

Marshmallow Snowman

As shown on page 110.

MATERIALS
- 3 jumbo marshmallows
- White frosting of choice
- 2 pretzel sticks
- 3 red hots
- 1 star sprinkle
- Toothpicks
- Black food coloring

INSTRUCTIONS
Place a small dab of frosting between the marshmallows and stack one atop the other. Poke a pretzel stick into opposite sides of the middle marshmallow to make snowman's arms.

Use small dabs of frosting to secure red hots down center of snowman for buttons and a star sprinkle for the nose.

Dip toothpick into black food coloring. Poke toothpick into top marshmallow to make the eyes and mouth.

symbols
of the
SEASON

All of your Christmas favorites come together in this chapter bringing you smiles and holiday pleasure. Those familiar faces and motifs that we look forward to seeing each year warm our hearts and fill our heads with charming gift–giving ideas and decorating fun.

Sure to become the holiday star, our Santa stocking uses many cherished holiday motifs—combining them all in brightly colored felt. Fill this cheerful stocking to the brim and personalize it with iron-on letters. Instructions and patterns for the stocking begin on page 121.

Design: Studio B

TRIO

Three all-time favorites—a snowman, a stocking, and a Christmas tree—
are all stitched up, made into ornaments, and then attached to a fresh green
wreath. We've added colorful skeins of floss to make the wreath a cross-stitcher's
choice. Instructions and patterns for the ornaments are on pages 126–128.

Design: Barbara Sestok

simple holly berry
VEST

Fun to wear and oh-so-easy to make, our holly vest is sure to be a crowd pleaser. The holly is cut and sewn onto the vest using the buttonhole stitch and the berries are added by sewing on bright red buttons. The edges of the vest are embellished with more stitches of holiday color. Instructions and patterns for the vest are on pages 128–129.

Design: Studio B

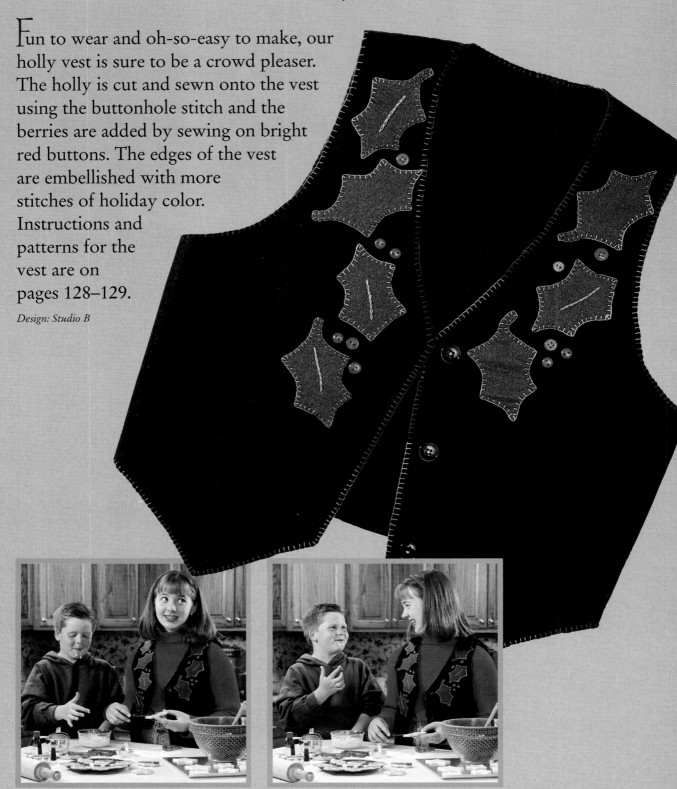

warm holidays
HOLLY
afghan

Snuggle by the fireside all wrapped up in our crocheted afghan made with worsted-weight yarn. The holly berries are crocheted bobbles that add dimension to this cozy winter throw. Instructions are on page 129.

Design: Ann E. Smith

santa family
WREATH

Santa has his whole family around him and they're dressed up for Christmas! Each member of the festive family is constructed from felt and embellished with simple stitches. We've attached the happy bunch to a grapevine wreath. Instructions and full-size patterns for the felt family are on pages 132–134.

Design: Studio B

tiny
CHRISTMAS
cross—stitch

Big stitching fun comes in little packages, and our mini Christmas pieces are no exception. Each tiny motif is stitched on perforated paper and then made into a tiny cone or trimmed to be used for napkin rings, package trims, or name cards. Instructions and charts for the pieces are on pages 134–135.

Design: Studio B

Santa Stocking

As shown on page 114, stocking measures 18×11 inches.

MATERIALS

Tracing paper; ½ yard of cream felt

9x12-inch piece *each* **of dark blue, light blue, orchid, medium purple, dark purple, gold, tan, white, black, red, pink, and green felt**

6x8-inch piece *each* **of yellow-green, gold, brown, purple, and turquoise cotton fabric**

Paper-backed double-sided fusible adhesive; pins

Cotton embroidery floss in colors to match felt; tapestry needle

Transfer paper and pen suitable for embroidery

Three ¼-inch-diameter buttons

INSTRUCTIONS

Enlarge and trace entire pattern piece 1 and stocking outline from diagram, *right,* onto tracing paper; cut out. Trace full-size numbered patterns, *pages 122–125,* onto tracing paper; cut out. Cut stocking front and back from cream felt. From dark blue felt, cut piece 1; from light blue, cut 2, 24, 38, and 42; from orchid, cut piece 3; from gold, cut 4, 5, 6, and 37; from dark purple, cut 8, 11, 12, and 36; from red, cut 9, 10, 27, 33, and 41; from tan, cut piece 15; from white, cut 7, 16, 17, 18, 19, 20, 23, and 24; from black, cut 21 and 22; from medium purple, cut 25 and 43; from green, cut 32 and 34; from pink, cut piece 35.

Fuse paper-backed adhesive to back of each cotton fabric, following manufacturer's instructions. Turn pattern pieces 13, 14, and 23 upside down onto back of yellow-green, trace onto paper backing and cut out. Repeat to cut pieces 26 and 29 from turquoise, 28 and 39 from gold, 30 and 31 from brown, and 40 from purple.

Pin piece 1 in place on stocking front, following diagram, *above.* Sew piece to stocking using appliqué stitch (see diagrams, *page 125*) and one ply of matching floss. Sew or fuse remaining pieces in numerical sequence, using appliqué stitch for pieces to be sewn. For hat (piece 10),

JACK-IN-THE-BOX PLACEMENT DIAGRAM **1 Square = 1 Inch**

refer to photograph, *page 114,* for shaping and position.

Use three plies of floss for all embroidery. Work running stitch using cream floss around edges of Santa's suit and hat. Using gold floss, work backstitch along "fold" lines of banner. Add light blue French knot to center of each drumstick head and work light blue blanket stitch around yellow-green fabric pinwheel pattern on ball. Couch strings hanging from stars in dark blue.

Transfer banner lettering, following manufacturer's instructions for transfer paper and pen. Backstitch then whipstitch over backstitch (see the

diagrams, *page 124*) lettering in dark blue. Add dots using French knots.

For name on stocking, write as desired and cut out from turquoise fabric; fuse to top front. If desired, name may be transferred to stocking using transfer paper and stitched.

Pin stocking front to back with wrong sides facing. Sew front to back using small whipstitches all around; leave top open.

Cut one 1¼×9½-inch strip and one ½×2½-inch strip from green felt. Wrap long strip around top edge of stocking; sew in place using appliqué stitch. Fold short strip in half; sew ends to top back corner for hanging loop.

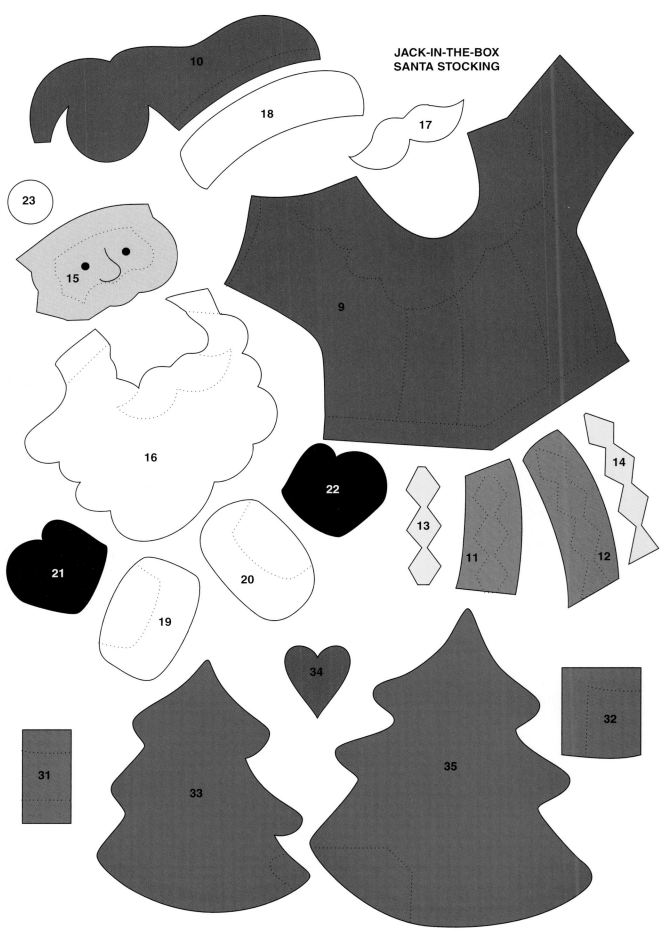

JACK-IN-THE-BOX SANTA STOCKING

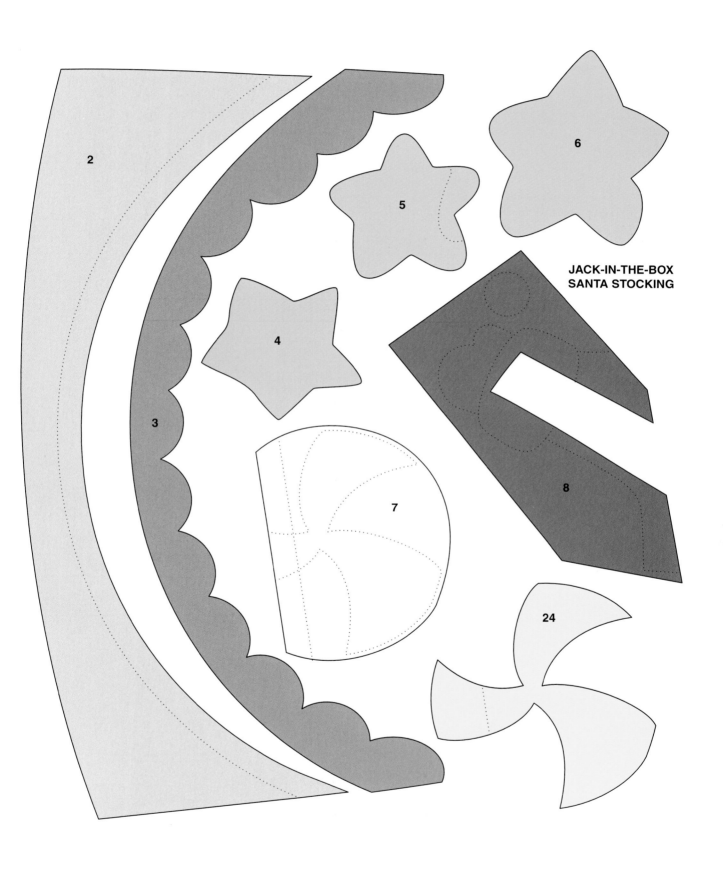

**JACK-IN-THE-BOX
SANTA STOCKING**

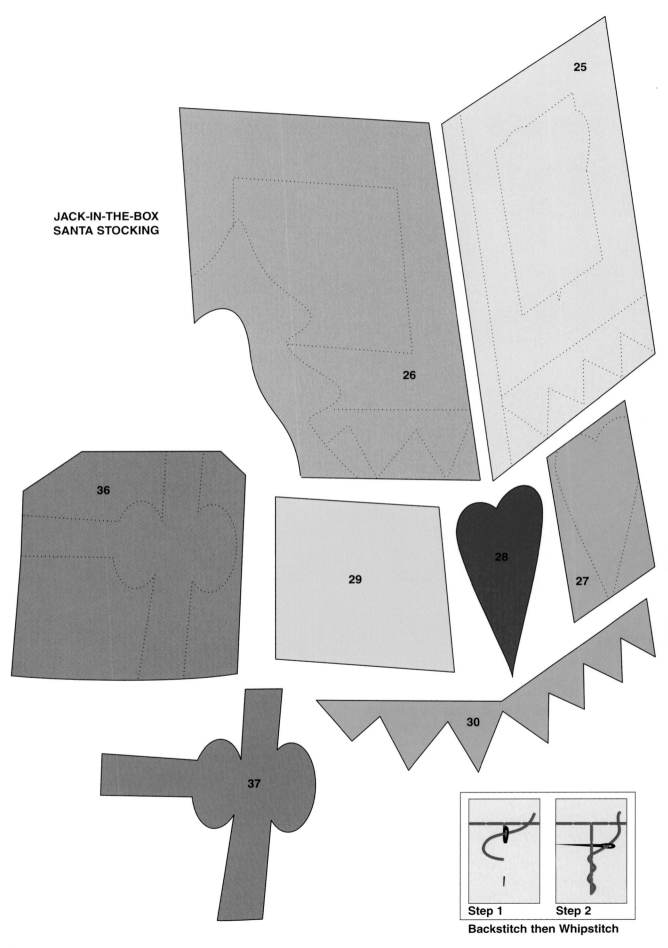

JACK-IN-THE-BOX
SANTA STOCKING

25

26

36

29

28

27

30

37

Step 1

Step 2

Backstitch then Whipstitch

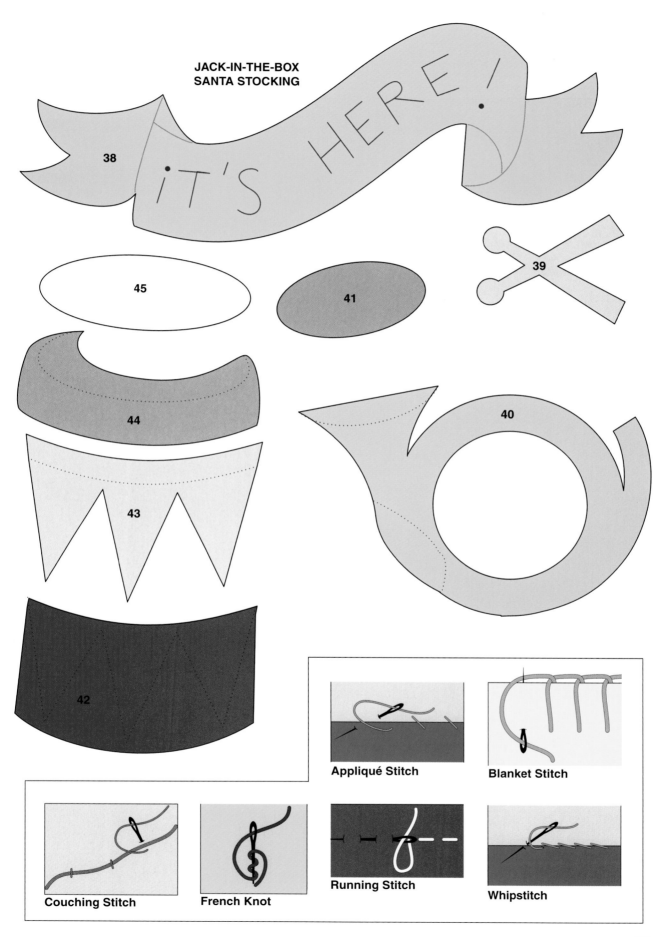

**JACK-IN-THE-BOX
SANTA STOCKING**

38

iT'S HERE !

45

41

39

44

43

40

42

Appliqué Stitch

Blanket Stitch

Couching Stitch

French Knot

Running Stitch

Whipstitch

Cross-Stitch Trio

As shown on page 115, finished ornaments measure from 6½ inches in diameter to 7×6 inches.

MATERIALS FOR ONE ORNAMENT
FABRICS
7x7-inch piece of 14-count white Aida cloth

7x7-inch piece of red, green, or white felt

FLOSS
Cotton embroidery floss in colors listed in key

Blending filament in colors listed in key

SUPPLIES
Needle; embroidery hoop

Beads in colors listed in key

Erasable fabric marker

7x7-inch piece of self-stick mounting board with foam

Tracing paper; crafts knife

½ yard of decorative sew-in piping in desired color

¾ yard of 1-inch-wide flat white or gold metallic cotton lace

12 inches of ¼-inch-wide satin ribbon in desired color; crafts glue

INSTRUCTIONS
Find the center of desired chart, *pages 127–128,* and center of fabric; begin stitching there. Use two plies of floss to work cross-stitches. Work blended needle as listed in key. Work all other stitches using one ply of floss or filament. Attach beads using one ply of floss.

Use fabric marker to draw outline around finished design in desired shape. Next, place tracing paper over stitched piece and lightly trace drawn outline; cut out tracing paper pattern. Place pattern on mounting board; trace around shape. Cut out mounting board shape with crafts knife. Cut matching back from felt.

Add 1-inch allowance around drawn outline of stitched piece; cut out. Peel protective paper from mounting board. Center foam side of mounting board on back of stitched design and press. Fold raw edges of Aida cloth to back; glue in place, clipping into fabric as necessary so it lies flat.

Glue piping around edge of ornament with piping seam allowance at back; overlap ends at bottom. Glue lace around ornament behind piping. For hanger, fold ribbon in half. Glue ends to top center of ornament. Glue felt to ornament back.

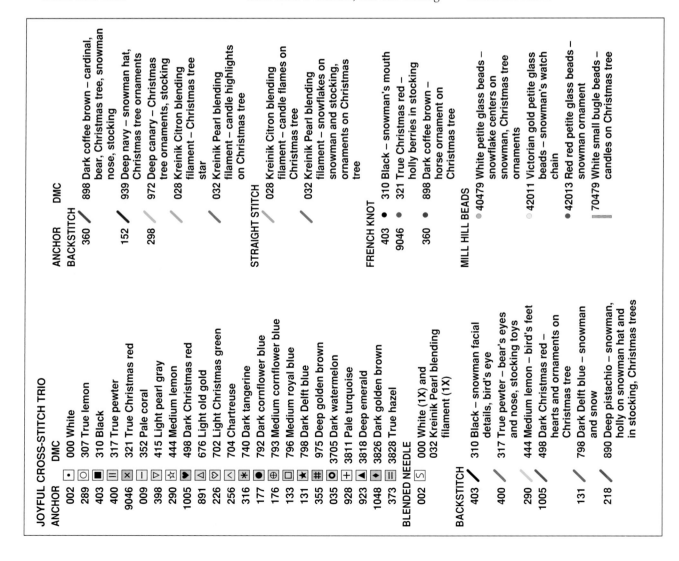

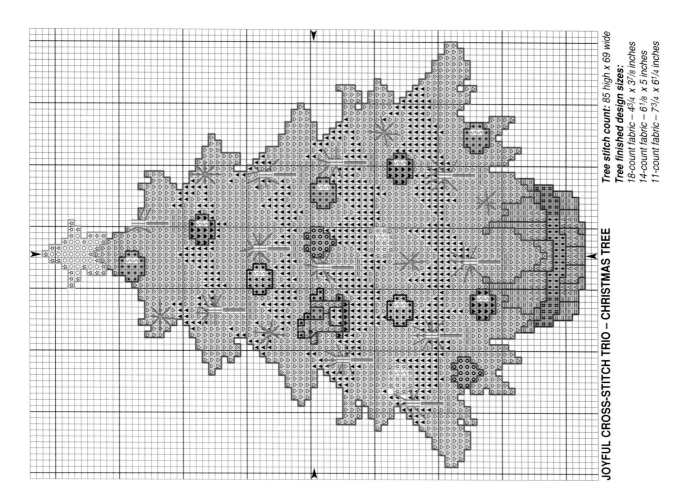

Tree stitch count: 85 high x 69 wide

Tree finished design sizes:
18-count fabric – 4³/₄ x 3⁷/₈ inches
14-count fabric – 6¹/₈ x 5 inches
11-count fabric – 7³/₄ x 6¹/₄ inches

JOYFUL CROSS-STITCH TRIO – CHRISTMAS TREE

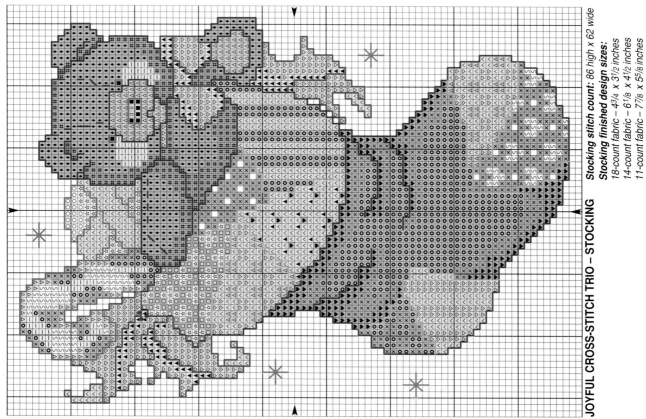

Stocking stitch count: 86 high x 62 wide

Stocking finished design sizes:
18-count fabric – 4³/₄ x 3¹/₂ inches
14-count fabric – 6¹/₈ x 4¹/₂ inches
11-count fabric – 7⁷/₈ x 5⁵/₈ inches

JOYFUL CROSS-STITCH TRIO – STOCKING

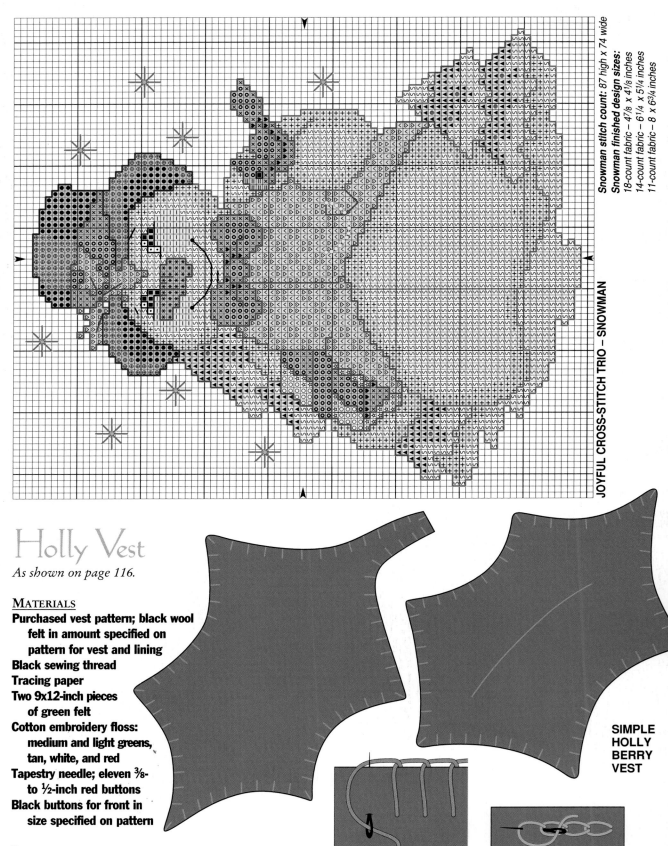

Snowman stitch count: 87 high x 74 wide
Snowman finished design sizes:
18-count fabric – 4⅞ x 4⅛ inches
14-count fabric – 6¼ x 5¼ inches
11-count fabric – 8 x 6¾ inches

Holly Vest

As shown on page 116.

MATERIALS

Purchased vest pattern; black wool felt in amount specified on pattern for vest and lining
Black sewing thread
Tracing paper
Two 9x12-inch pieces of green felt
Cotton embroidery floss: medium and light greens, tan, white, and red
Tapestry needle; eleven ⅜- to ½-inch red buttons
Black buttons for front in size specified on pattern

INSTRUCTIONS

Using pattern, cut vest and identical lining pieces from felt. For both vest and lining, sew fronts to backs at shoulders and sides. Set lining aside.

Blanket Stitch

Chain Stitch

SIMPLE HOLLY BERRY VEST

Trace holly leaves, *above,* onto tracing paper; cut out. From green felt, cut five leaves with stems and two leaves without stems. Pin leaves as desired onto vest front, using photograph, *page 116,* as a guide.

Sew leaves to vest using blanket stitch, *page 128*, and two plies of floss. Use two plies of light green to work a chain stitch vein down center of desired leaves. Alternate floss colors as desired around each leaf. Using green floss, sew red buttons among leaves for berries.

Pin lining to vest, wrong sides facing. Sew lining to vest around all edges, using two plies of floss and blanket stitch. Alternate floss colors as desired while stitching.

Make buttonholes and attach buttons as specified on pattern.

Holly Afghan

As shown on page 117, afghan measures approximately 47×60 inches.

SKILL LEVEL
For the intermediate crocheter

MATERIALS
Red Heart with wool worsted-weight yarn (6-oz./170-gm. skein): three skeins *each* of hunter green (589) and tan (535); one skein of wine (576)
Size 8/H (5.00 mm) aluminum crochet hook or size to obtain gauge
Yarn needle

GAUGE
In dc and color pattern, 12 sts = 4 inches; 10 rows = 7 inches.

INSTRUCTIONS
Note: The holly motif is worked from the chart, right, reading from right to left for RS rows and from left to right for WS rows. Use butterflies or separate bobbins for each color. To change color in dc, in last st before next color work the dc until 2 loops remain on hook, with new color yo and complete the dc. Berry bobbles and stems are added to each finished block.
First Block: Beginning at the lower edge with tan, ch 51.

Row 1 (RS): Dc in fourth ch from hook and in each ch across = 49 dc; turn.

Row 2: Ch 3 (counts as dc); dc in each dc across following chart for color changes; turn.

Rows 3–19: Rep Row 2. Fasten off after Row 19.

Border, Rnd 1: With the RS facing, join tan with a sl st in top dc at right edge. Ch 1, 3 sc in same st, sc in each of next 47 sts, 3 sc in next st, work 38 sc evenly spaced along edge, 3 sc in corner, working along opposite edge of foundation ch, sc in each of next 47 ch, 3 sc in next ch, work 38 sc evenly spaced along edge; join with sl st in first sc and fasten off.

Rnd 2: With the RS facing, join wine with sl st in center sc of top right corner. Ch 1, 3 sc in same sc, sc in each sc around working 3 sc in center sc of each corner; at end, sl st in front lp of first sc.

Rnd 3: Sl st in front lp of each sc around. Fasten off.

Rnd 4: With the RS facing, join green with sl st in sixth rem lp from top right corner. Ch 3 (counts as dc), working in rem lps from Rnd 2, dc in each of next 40 lps; for corner, (ch 2, sk 2 lps, 5 dc in next lp) 3 times, ch 2, sk 2 lps; for side, dc in each of next 32 lps; rep corner as est, dc in each of next 41 lps, rep corner as est, dc in each of next 32 lps, rep corner as est; join with sl in third ch of beg ch-3.

Rnd 5: Ch 3 (counts as dc); dc in each of next 40 dc; for corner (ch 3, dc2tog, dc in next dc, dc2tog) 3 times, ch 3; dc in each of next 32 dc, rep corner, dc in each of next 41 dc, rep corner, dc in each of next 32 dc, rep corner; join with sl st in 3rd ch of beg ch-3.

Rnd 6: Ch 3 (counts as dc), dc in each of next 40 dc; for corner [ch 1, (dc3tog, ch 4, sc in ch-3 lp, ch 4) twice, dc3tog, ch 1]; dc in each of next 32 dc, rep corner, dc in each of next 41 dc, rep corner, dc in each of next 32 dc, rep corner; join with sl st in 3rd ch of beginning ch-3. Fasten off.

Bobble: Locating berry bobbles as shown on the chart, with the RS facing join wine with sl st over dc post, ch 1. Working over same dc post, (yo and draw up a lp) 4 times, yo and draw through all 9 lps on hook, ch 1 to close. Fasten off. Draw tails to WS of fabric; secure in place.

Leaf Vein: With the RS facing, join green with sl st in leaf corner; loosely sl st in a diagonal line using the chart as a guide. Fasten off. Weave in loose ends on WS of fabric.

Finishing: Make five more Blocks as for the First. Join together in three pairs by whip-stitching through front lps with green; then join the pairs together.

Edging: With the RS facing, join wine with sl st in ch-1 sp to right of any corner ivy group. Ch 1, sc in same sp, (5 sc in top of leaf, 3 sc in ch-4 lp, sc in sc, 3 sc in next ch-4 lp) twice, 5 sc in top of next leaf, sc in ch-1 sp, sc in each dc to next ch-1 sp, sc in ch-1 sp, 5 sc in top of next leaf, 3 sc in ch-4 lp, sc in sc, 3 sc in next ch-4 lp, sc in top of next 2 leaves at joining, 3 sc in next ch-4 lp, sc in sc, 3 sc in next ch-4 lp, 5 sc in top of next leaf, sc in ch-1 sp, sc in each dc to corner; rep as est around entire afghan; at end, join with sl st in first sc and fasten off.

WARM HOLIDAYS HOLLY AFGHAN
☐ Beige
☒ Green
BERRY BOBBLE PLACEMENT
⊜ Red
LEAF VEIN PLACEMENT
╲ Green

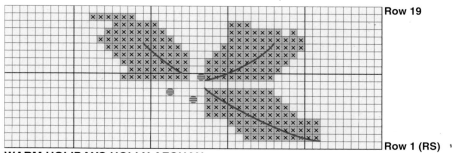

WARM HOLIDAYS HOLLY AFGHAN

Row 19

Row 1 (RS)

Sweet Sherrie the Sugar Plum Fairy

As shown on page 118, finished doll is 12½ inches tall.

MATERIALS
Tracing paper
¼ yard of pink brushed flannel or knit fabric
8x5-inch piece of purple print cotton fabric
13x5-inch piece of purple velveteen
Scrap of green felt
Scrap of dark pink felt
Fabric marking pen for light fabric
Fabric marking pencil for dark fabric
2x5-inch piece of posterboard
Gold spray paint
Sewing thread: pink, light green, and gold
Carpet thread: white and black
Polyester fiberfill
½ yard of ¼-inch-wide gold metallic trim
20 inches of ⅛-inch-wide gold metallic ribbon
Gold glitter paint; fabric glue
Hot-glue gun; pins
2 black seed beads; nubby gold yarn
7x2-inch piece of stiff cardboard
16x11-inch piece of purple tulle
Large gold star nailhead
Scrap of tissue paper
Cosmetic powder blush
18-inch-long piece of 20-gauge white cloth-covered wire
Clear plastic wrap; hair dryer; gold glitter
Six ¼-inch clear acrylic star gems

INSTRUCTIONS
Trace patterns, right and *pages 131–132,* onto tracing paper and cut out. Cut 8x7-inch piece of pink fabric. Layer pink fabric on top of purple print, and sew the two together along one 8-inch side. Open fabric out and refold widthwise, right sides facing. Position body pattern on folded fabric with marked waistline along fabric seam. Draw around body pattern using fabric marker; *do not* cut out.

Fold remaining pink fabric and purple velveteen in half with right sides facing. Use fabric marker to draw around arm pattern twice, and head pattern once onto flannel. Draw around skirt pattern once onto velveteen.

Sew around drawn outlines on doubled fabrics, leaving openings as marked on patterns. Cut out pieces ¼ inch beyond stitching; clip curves. Stuff each piece, except skirt, firmly and sew openings closed.

Cut leaves from green felt. Trace mouth from face pattern and cut from dark pink felt. Spray front and back of posterboard gold. When paint is dry, cut crown from posterboard.

For skirt, turn under top and bottom raw edges ⅛ inch; stitch. Using black carpet thread, run hand gathering stitch around bottom edge. Slip skirt up over legs and pull thread to gather skirt around legs above knees. Knot thread to secure. Stuff skirt firmly through top opening. Gather skirt top in same manner, adjust gathers around waist, and knot thread to secure. Tack skirt top edge to waist. Cut shoulder straps from flat gold trim; glue in place.

Paint slippers on feet using gold glitter paint and pattern as a guide. Cut ribbon length in half. When paint is dry, dot glue at center of each ribbon length and pin center to leg seam at dot on pattern. When glue is dry, wrap ribbon around leg, criss-cross in front, then back, and bring ends back around to front to knot at ankle. Trim ends.

Sew bead eyes to face using black thread. To hide knots, enter and exit from back of head for all face detail. Using single strand of black thread, complete eyes and nose as shown on

pattern. Glue mouth in place. Detail mouth using black straight stitches.

Pin top of neck to back of head ⅓ of way up from bottom edge. Whipstitch top and sides of neck to head back.

For hair, cut 2½x2½-inch square from pink fabric. Wrap nubby yarn lengthwise around cardboard rectangle to make thick bunch of hair. (Number of wraps depends on thickness of yarn.) Slide yarn carefully off cardboard and center across fabric square. Machine stitch down center of square, securing yarn. Trim fabric to ¼ inch on each side of stitching. Glue fabric strip down center of head, beginning just above eyebrows. When glue is dry, tack yarn loops to head at random.

For tutu, fold tulle in half lengthwise, and in half again. Pin edges together to secure. Using black carpet thread, hand gather double folded edge. Pull gathering thread and fit tutu around waist. Knot threads; adjust gathers. Glue remaining flat gold trim around waist for waistband. Pull apart netting layers to fluff tutu.

Glue arms to shoulders so arms curve toward front. Position each leaf on tissue paper scrap; machine stitch leaf veins using green thread. Remove tissue backing. Glue two leaves to top of one arm at shoulder and remaining leaf to bodice. Glue star nailhead to bodice at center. Add rosy cheeks to face using cosmetic blush.

For wings, use wing outline pattern and beginning at dot, bend wire into wing shape. Twist ends together around center, leaving enough at one end to make tiny loop to extend above center section. Cut off excess wire.

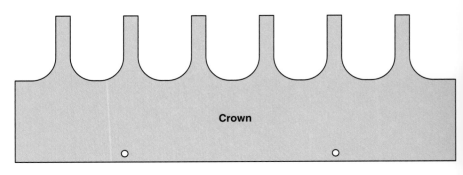

Crown

Cut two 7×12-inch pieces of plastic wrap. Center one side of wings frame on one side of plastic. Pull plastic over wing; gather edges tightly at center point of wings. Use hair dryer to heat plastic, shrinking it over wire frame. Cut off excess plastic at center. Repeat for other side of wings. Wrap white carpet thread several times around center, criss-crossing as necessary to secure plastic ends. Sew loop on wings to back of doll's body.

Brush crown lightly with glue; sprinkle with glitter. Glue acrylic star to each point. Overlap ends of crown; glue. Hot-glue long straight pins to inside bottom edge at dots, with points extending down beyond crown edge. Push pins into head top to secure crown. If doll is to be handled by children, omit pins and hot-glue crown directly to head.

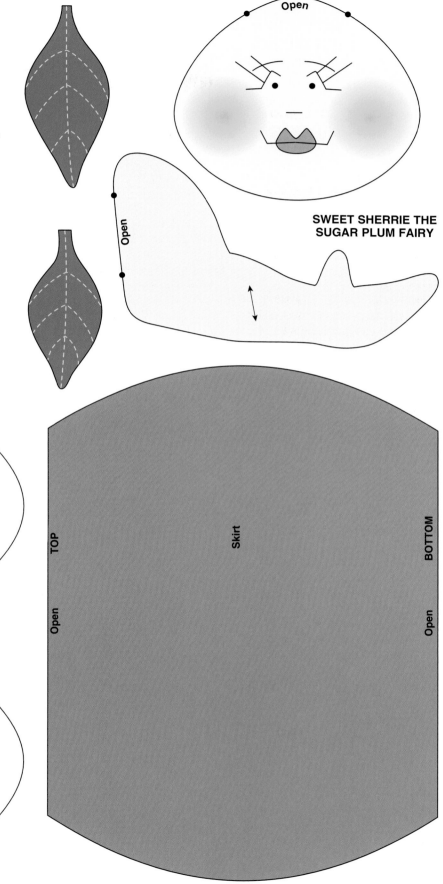

Open

SWEET SHERRIE THE SUGAR PLUM FAIRY

Open

Wings

TOP

Open

Skirt

BOTTOM

Open

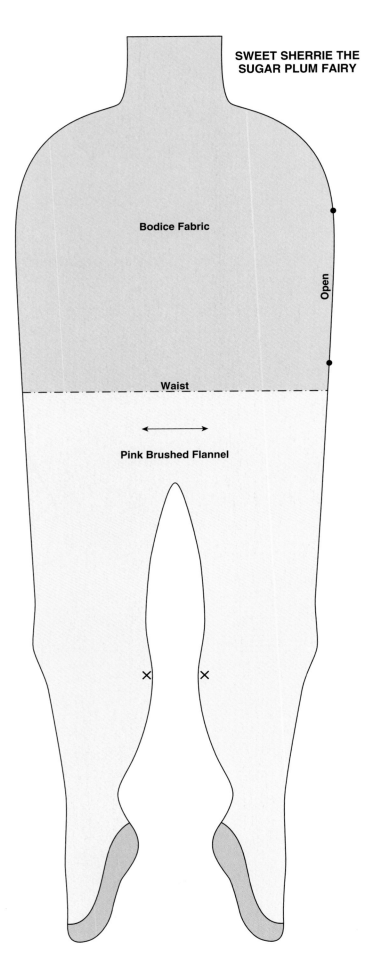

SWEET SHERRIE THE SUGAR PLUM FAIRY

Bodice Fabric

Open

Waist

Pink Brushed Flannel

✕ ✕

Santa Family Wreath

As shown on page 119, figures range from 3¾ to 5½ inches tall.

MATERIALS
Tracing paper
9x11-inch piece *each* of charcoal, medium gray, deep blue, burgundy, purple, white, and cream felt
Fusible web
Cotton embroidery floss: gray, black, burgundy, white, cream, lavender, and purple
Five ⅜-inch white buttons
1 yard of ³⁄₁₆-inch-wide navy blue soutache braid
12-inch-diameter grapevine wreath
Hot-glue gun (optional)

INSTRUCTIONS
Trace patterns, *pages 133–134,* onto tracing paper; cut out. Cut two entire shapes for each figure from fusible web. Cut individual parts from felt using cream for faces and hands, white for beard and hat pom-poms, and felt colors as desired for remainder of pieces. (The photograph, *page 119,* may be used for ideas.) Cut Santa's suit without cutouts for placket and pocket; these will be fused on top of felt suit piece. Reserve remaining felt for backing pieces.

For Santa, use scraps of fusible web to fuse placket and pockets in place on suit, following the manufacturer's instructions for web.

For each figure, lay one fusible web shape onto felt backing. Arrange felt pieces on top of web according to pattern. Fuse pieces to

**SANTA FAMILY
WREATH**

backing. Cut out
backing around the figure.

Following pattern, add stitching
using three plies of floss. (See
diagrams, *page 134.*) Use
matching floss for running
stitches on faces, hands, and
for blanket stitching around
beard. Work facial features,
including French knot
mouths, using black. Stitch
heart on Santa baby using
burgundy floss and satin
stitch. Use contrasting
colors as desired for all
other stitches.

Use second web shape
to fuse each figure to another
matching backing piece; cut
out. Whipstitch the backing
pieces together around the outside
edges using floss to match the felt.

Sew buttons to dots on figures
as shown on the patterns. Cut
4 inches of soutache braid; tie in a
bow. Tack the bow to the front of
Mrs. Santa's jumper.

Cut 6 inches of braid for each
figure. Fold each piece in half, join
ends, and sew to top back of figure
for hanging loop.

If desired, use hot glue gun to
affix each figure to wreath as
shown in photograph, *page 119.*

SANTA FAMILY WREATH

As shown on page 120, finished trims measure from 2⅝×2¼ inches to 3×2⅜ inches.

MATERIALS FOR ONE TRIM
FABRIC
4x3-inch piece of 14-count white perforated paper
FLOSS
Cotton embroidery floss in colors listed in key
SUPPLIES
Needle

INSTRUCTIONS
Find the center of the desired chart, *opposite*, and the center of the perforated paper; begin stitching there. Use two plies of floss to work cross-stitches and French knots. Work backstitches using one ply of floss.

Trim completed stitchery as shown on chart to form a cone, if desired. If a cone is not desired, trim one square beyond all stitches. To secure a cone shape, stitch or glue the ends together.

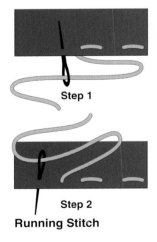

Step 1

Step 2

Running Stitch

French Knot

Satin Stitch Heart

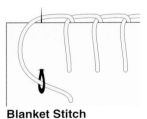

Blanket Stitch

TINY CHRISTMAS CROSS-STITCH		
ANCHOR		DMC
002	·	000 White
403	■	310 Black
9046	⊙	321 Christmas red
009	⁄	352 Coral
008	#	353 Peach
046	♡	666 Red
923	★	699 Christmas green
128	+	775 Baby blue
131	▲	798 Dark Delft blue
130	S	809 True Delft blue
1005	◆	816 Garnet
204	=	913 Nile green
306	●	3820 Straw
BACKSTITCH		
936	⁄	632 Cocoa – snowman's wreath and Santa's beard
403	⁄	310 Black – all remaining backstitches
FRENCH KNOT		
403	●	310 Black – angel's eyes, snowman's eyes and mouth

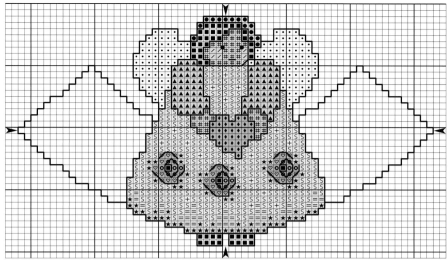

Angel stitch count: *37 high x 31 wide*
Angel finished design sizes:
14-count plastic – 2⅝ x 2¼ inches
7-count plastic – 5¼ x 4½ inches
10-count plastic – 3¾ x 3⅛ inches

TINY CHRISTMAS CROSS-STITCH – ANGEL

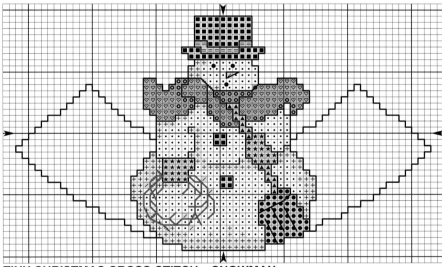

Snowman stitch count: *38 high x 29 wide*
Snowman finished design sizes:
14-count plastic – 2¾ x 2 inches
7-count plastic – 5½ x 4⅛ inches
10-count plastic – 3⅞ x 3 inches

TINY CHRISTMAS CROSS-STITCH – SNOWMAN

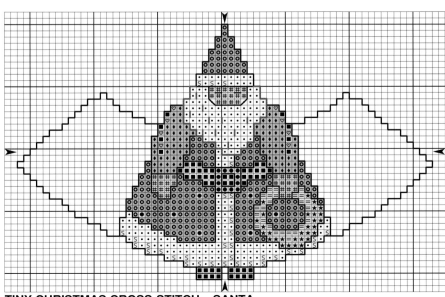

Santa stitch count: *41 high x 33 wide*
Santa finished design sizes:
14-count plastic – 3 x 2⅜ inches
7-count plastic – 5⅞ x 4¾ inches
10-count plastic – 4⅛ x 3⅜ inches

TINY CHRISTMAS CROSS-STITCH – SANTA

CHRISTMAS house-warming

Every part of your house will sparkle with the colors of Christmas when you fill it with thoughtful touches of this giving season. From the ornaments on the tree to the chairs around the table, we've gathered some irresistible ideas to fill your house with love and holiday excitement.

jolly felt
BANNER

Portrayed in colorful felt, our playful banner sets the stage for a happy holiday. The pieces are all cut from felt, then sewn to a background piece. Simple stitches display the sweet saying. Instructions and patterns begin on page 145.

Design: Studio B

my special peppermint
CHAIRS

Tiny well-worn chairs found in the attic were magically
transformed into very special holiday chairs for the youngest
Christmas lover using just a little paint and imagination.
Sure to be brought out every year, these peppermint-striped
works of art have traditional messages written across the top.
Instructions and ideas for painting the chairs are on page 150.

Design: Alice Wetzel

regal beaded
ORNAMENT

A simple Christmas ball takes on a royal duty when topped with glass beads. The beadwork slips over the top of the ball and can fit most any size ornament. Instructions for the ornament are on page 151.

Design: Phyllis Dobbs

quilted snowflake
STOCKING

Quilted with a variety of royal blue fabrics in icicle-shaped pieces, our snowflake stocking is a show-stopper. After the body of the stocking is pieced, the cuff is added displaying elegant white woolen snowflakes embellished with iridescent sequins. Instructions and patterns begin on page 152.

Design: Margaret Sindelar

christmas FLORALS
tree skirt

Silken stitches of various embroidery techniques make this tree skirt a treasured heirloom. Poinsettias, jade leaves, and delicate florals weave their way around this exquisite piece. Instructions are on pages 154–156.

Design: Phyllis Dobbs

BERIBBONED
trim

Scraps of ribbon, tiny stitches, and shiny beads line up to form a most striking Christmas trim. The ribbon scraps are fused to the background fabric and then embellished with favorite embroidery stitches. Instructions for the ornament are on page 156.

Design: Margaret Sindelar

whimsical
PAINTED
chair

This lonely chair had a happy ending with playful winter motifs painted upon it. Tiny purchased wood shapes were painted, strung, and tied to the back of the chair to make it a favorite. Instructions and tips are on page 157.

Design: Alice Wetzel

christmas
ROSE
chair

A flea-market chair with a common rose pattern takes on a new life with some special painting techniques. Coated with layers of color and spattered with tiny dots of paint, the piece is transformed into a holiday work of art. Step-by-step instructions are on page 158.

Design: Alice Wetzel

Jolly Felt Banner

As shown on page 138, wallhanging is 15¾×18½ inches.

MATERIALS
Tracing paper
15x18-inch piece of black felt
9x12-inch piece *each* **of light ivory, cream, gold, light blue, turquoise, green, bright pink, lavender, purple, orchid, and dusty blue felt**
Scrap *each* **of gold, light brown, dark brown, and tan felt**
17x18¼-inch piece of light blue felt
Pins
Cotton embroidery floss in colors to match felt, including navy blue
Tapestry needle
14¾x5-inch piece of light blue broadcloth
14¾x5-inch piece of fusible web
Transfer paper and pen suitable for embroidery patterns
21-inch-long, ⅜-inch-diameter wood wallhanging dowel
Black acrylic paint; paintbrush
27 inches of black nylon cord

INSTRUCTIONS
Trace numbered pattern pieces, *pages 146–148,* onto tracing paper; cut out. From ivory felt, cut pieces 14, 28, 29, 32, 33, 34, 38, and 45; from cream, cut 8, 24, 26, and 35; from gold, cut 31; from light blue, cut 12, 23, 37, and 47; from turquoise, cut 1, 11, and 13; from green, cut 5, 6, and 7; from bright pink, cut 30, 36, 39, 40, 41, 42, and 44; from lavender, cut 21, 22, and 25; from purple, cut 2, 9, 10, 48, 49, and 50; from orchid, cut 3, 18, 43, and 46; from dusty blue, cut 4; from light brown, cut 15, 19, and 20; from dark brown, cut 16 and 17; and from tan, cut 27.

Pin piece 1 in place on black felt, following placement diagram, *right.* Sew piece to black felt using appliqué stitch and one ply of matching floss. In same manner, pin and stitch pieces 2 through 50, in numerical sequence.

Fuse broadcloth rectangle in place on felt following manufacturer's

instructions for fusible web. Trace lettering and heart from pattern onto tracing paper. Turn tracing upside down and trace onto transfer paper using transfer pen. Following the manufacturer's instructions, transfer lettering to broadcloth.

Backstitch, then whipstitch lettering using three plies of navy blue floss. Using three plies of bright pink floss, satin stitch heart. Work blanket stitch around edges of broadcloth using three plies of light blue floss.

Center entire design on top of light blue felt rectangle with top edge of black felt 1½ inches from top edge of blue felt. Sew pieces together around perimeter ¾ inch from outer edges of black felt using running stitch and two plies of black floss. Cut free-hand scallop pattern around edges of black felt.

Cut notches in top of light blue felt according to notch diagram, *below.* Turn resulting three tabs to back and whipstitch edges to running stitch seam line.

Cut two ½×13-inch strips each from bright pink, lavender, purple, and orchid felt. Align one strip of each color; knot in center. Repeat to make two tassels. Tack one tassel to each bottom corner; trim ends.

Paint dowel black; allow to dry. Slide dowel through tabs on wallhanging. Knot each end of cord around one end of dowel to hang.

**JOLLY FELT BANNER
PLACEMENT DIAGRAM**

**JOLLY FELT BANNER
NOTCH DIAGRAM**

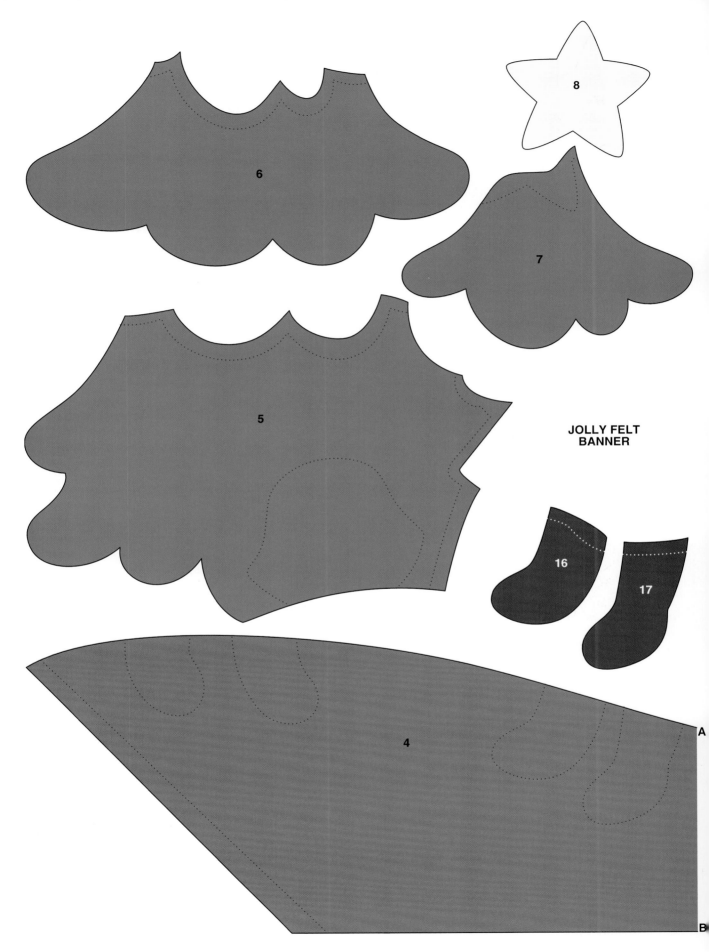

JOLLY FELT
BANNER

JOLLY FELT
BANNER

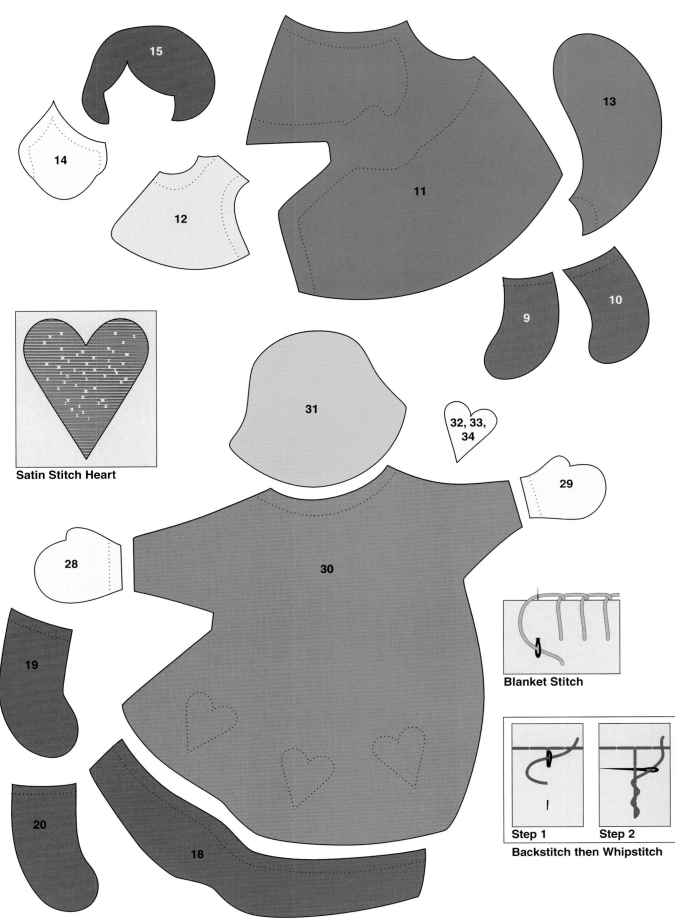

Satin Stitch Heart

Blanket Stitch

Step 1 Step 2

Backstitch then Whipstitch

Tis The La-La

Season La-La

to be

La-La

Jolly

♥

1, 2, 3

fa-La-La

La-La

Peppermint Chairs

As shown on page 139.

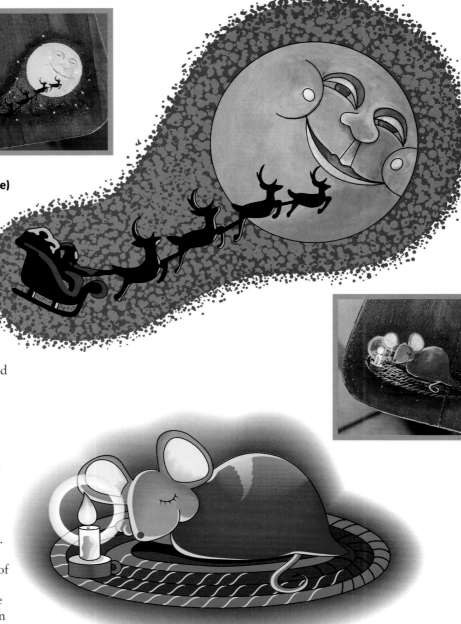

MATERIALS
Child's wood chair
Sandpaper; tack cloth
Acrylic wood primer (for painted base)
Wood stain (for stained base)
Acrylic paints in desired colors
**Paintbrushes; small natural
    cosmetic sponge**
Drafting tape; pencil
Clear acrylic spray varnish

INSTRUCTIONS

Sand surfaces to prepare; wipe with tack cloth. For new wood to be painted, apply coat of primer; allow to dry. Apply desired base color to each section. Apply second coat if necessary and allow to dry. For wood to be stained, apply according to manufacturer's instructions; allow to dry.

Refer to photographs, *page 139*, for design ideas. For spokes, paint a variety of geometric or freehand designs, using several colors. Use tape as a mask and guide as necessary to create blocks of color. Add stripes of contrasting color; make polka dots using eraser end of pencil dipped in paint.

For moon and sleigh design, use pattern, *top right*, as a guide. Begin by creating background using thinned dark blue paint. Sponge this mixture onto wood lightly, allowing some of wood to show through. Add lighter blue layer on top of dark blue, covering lightly. For stars, dip end of brush handle in yellow and dot onto background. Add smaller dot of ivory on top of yellow. Paint moon using ivory and soft gray-blue. Use slightly more blue in shaded areas, working colors together while still wet. Highlight eyelids, nose, cheeks, and bottom lip using more ivory. Paint sleigh and reindeer black. Highlight using red and light peach or ivory.

For sleepy mouse design, use pattern, *above,* as a guide. Sponge a translucent background as for moon, *above*. Paint mouse using soft gray; highlight using lighter gray. Paint blanket red; shade with tiny bit of dark blue. Highlight blanket using thinned yellow paint. For rug, paint using a darker color (deep blue or dark green) topped with a sponged application of a lighter color (turquoise or lime green). Paint candle white with a yellow and orange flame. Make glow around flame using soft

yellow thinned to transparency, adding layers of paint until desired effect is achieved. Finish by highlighting mouse, blanket, and rug with same thinned yellow paint and very fine brush.

Paint messages across top of the chair, if desired. *(Note: We wrote the phrases, "'Twas the night before Christmas when all through the house..." and "Happy Christmas to all...and to all a good night!")*

After all paint is thoroughly dry, spray the entire chair with clear acrylic varnish.

Regal Beaded Ornament

As shown on page 140.

MATERIALS

2-inch-diameter glass ball ornament
Red glass seed beads
Red and green small glass
   bugle beads
Red beading or quilting thread
Beading needle; scissors

INSTRUCTIONS

Cut a 36-inch length of thread. String one seed bead onto thread, slide to 1 inch from end, and tie knot around bead. This will hold other beads on thread. String 40 seed beads. (See Step 1, *above right*.) Make circle by going through first bead strung after knot bead, then taking needle through first 30 beads. (See Step 2.)

Bring needle out, as shown in Step 3, and string seven seed beads. String two red bugle beads. Go back through both bugle beads again in same direction, pulling beads close side by side. String another bugle bead and go back through prior bead and again through last bead. Continue until eight bugle beads have been strung. Pull close after each addition.

After eighth bugle bead, string fringe consisting of two seed beads, one green bugle bead, three seed beads, one green bugle bead, three seed beads, one green bugle bead, and three seed beads. (See Step 4.) Take needle back through fringe, starting with last green bugle bead strung. The last three seed beads will form a loop. When top of fringe is reached, go back through last red bugle bead. Repeat to make another fringe on opposite side of bugle bead from first fringe. After fringe is completed, go back and forth through red bugle beads, working up to top bugle bead. The needle should come out on opposite side from where the seven seed beads were strung.

String seven seed beads. Go through eighth bead from starting point after making first circle. (See second illustration in Step 4.) String another seven seed beads and continue as directed, *above,* to make a second fringe unit. Repeat for a total of five fringe units. End thread by weaving back through several beads and making a small knot around thread where you exit. Weave through a few more beads; clip thread.

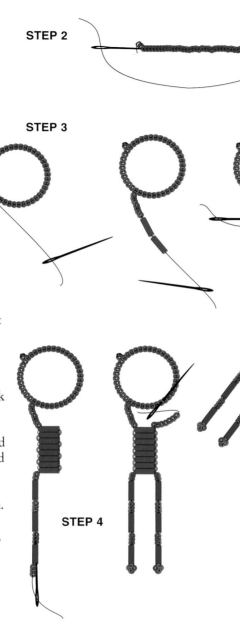

STEP 1

STEP 2

STEP 3

STEP 4

STEP 5

Start a new thread by securing and weaving down through a unit of red bugle beads. Come out one side of a bottom red bugle bead and string 17 seed beads. Go through bottom red bugle bead of adjacent fringe unit. String 17 seed beads and repeat until reaching starting point.

Run thread back through bottom red bugle beads and string second row with 22 beads in each section. Repeat with third row of 29 beads in each section. If bottom bugle bead becomes too tight, go through next bugle bead above. Do not pull beads in second and third strings too tight; allow them to be loose enough so beads do not overlap beads at ends of other strings. Strings should lay flat against each other. End thread.

Remove cap from top of ornament. Slip finished beading over top or ornament; replace cap.

Quilted Snowflake Stocking

As shown on page 141, stocking measures 18½×10½ inches.

MATERIALS

Fabric yardages are for 45-inch-wide fabrics
Graph paper
Twelve assorted 3x5-inch pieces of royal blue taffeta fabrics
½ yard of medium weight royal blue wool
½ yard of royal blue lining fabric
¼ yard of medium-heavy weight royal blue wool
8x18-inch piece of white wool
20x12-inch piece of fleece
1½ yard of gold metallic piping
Royal blue sewing thread
Paper-backed iron-on adhesive
Rayon machine embroidery thread: white and royal blue
Tear-away fabric stabilizer
6 inches of gold metallic cord
30 clear crystal medium bugle beads
5 clear crystal large bugle beads
3 blue and 3 crystal ³⁄₁₆-inch flower-shaped beads
¾-inch-diameter crystal star charm
18-inch-long white cord with tassel ends or 18 inches of 1½-inch-wide white ribbon

INSTRUCTIONS

Enlarge stocking and cuff patterns, *page 154*, onto graph paper; cut out. Trace triangle piece pattern, *page 153*, onto tracing paper and cut out. Patterns include ¼-inch seam allowances. Cut stocking back from medium weight blue wool, stocking front and back from lining, cuff from medium-heavy blue wool, and seventy triangles from assorted taffeta fabrics.

Sew seams with right sides of fabric facing unless otherwise indicated. Use ¼-inch seam allowances for piecing stocking front and ½-inch seam allowances for stocking construction.

Sew triangles together in pairs, matching long sides to form thirty-five slanted rectangles. Sew rectangles together along long sides to make five strips of seven rectangles. Sew long sides of strips together to make a large rectangle. Cut stocking front from pieced fabric. Cut fleece to match stocking front; baste to wrong side, ½ inch from edges. Sew piping to stocking front around sides and bottom along basting line. Sew stocking front to back. Clip and trim seam; turn to right side.

Trace snowflakes, *below* and *page 153*, onto paper side of fusible adhesive. Fuse to wrong side of white wool and cut out. Using photograph, *page 141*, as a guide, arrange snowflakes on cuff beginning at center front. Trim away excess snowflake extending beyond top edge; allow middle snowflake to extend beyond bottom edge. Back cuff with fabric stabilizer and using short, narrow zigzag stitches, machine appliqué snowflakes to cuff around edges. Stitch around extended edges of

middle snowflake onto fabric stabilizer. Using blue machine embroidery thread, work same stitch around bottom edge of cuff. Cut or tear away fabric stabilizer.

Sew ends of cuff together for center back seam. Baste cuff to stocking top edge, wrong side of cuff facing right side of stocking. Ease cuff top edge as necessary to fit stocking; stitch. For hanger, fold gold cord in half; sew ends together at top of outside seam, matching ends to fabric raw edges.

Sew lining front to back, leaving opening in bottom of foot for turning. Slip stocking into lining with wrong sides facing. Align side seams and stitch around top edge. Pull stocking to right side through opening in lining. Sew opening closed. Smooth lining down into stocking. Turn cuff up and topstitch around top opening edge, keeping cuff free.

Follow snowflake patterns, *pages 152–153*, for bead and charm placement; sew in place.

Tie cord or ribbon into a bow. Tack the bow to the stocking at the seam below the hanging loop.

**QUILTED
SNOWFLAKE
STOCKING
PIECING
TRIANGLE**

QUILTED SNOWFLAKE STOCKING

Medium bugle beads

Large bugle beads

Flower-shaped beads

Star charm

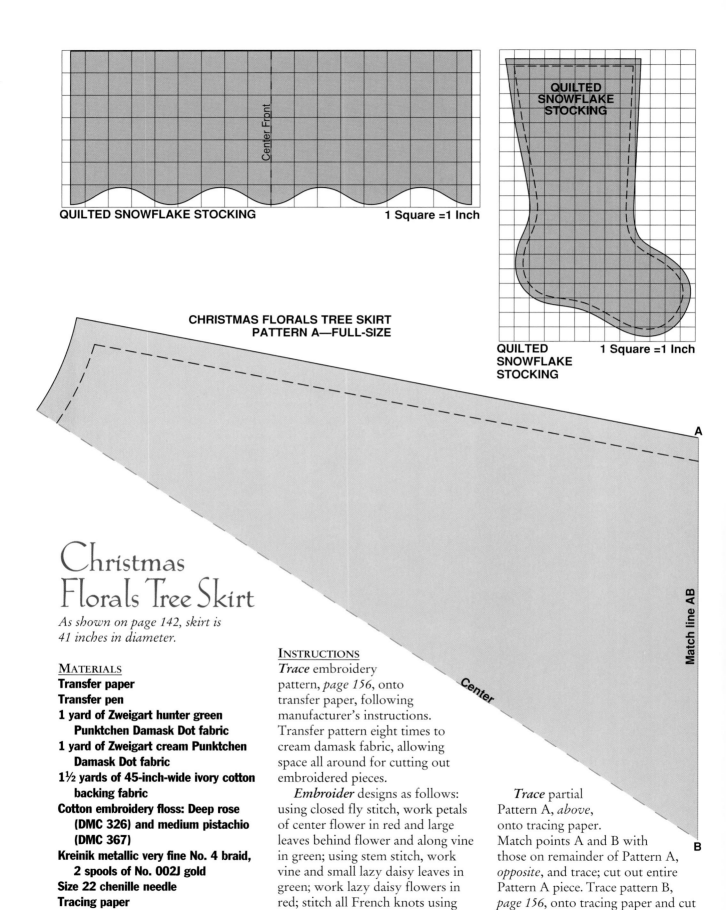

QUILTED SNOWFLAKE STOCKING

Center Front

QUILTED SNOWFLAKE STOCKING   1 Square =1 Inch

QUILTED SNOWFLAKE STOCKING

QUILTED
SNOWFLAKE
STOCKING   1 Square =1 Inch

**CHRISTMAS FLORALS TREE SKIRT
PATTERN A—FULL-SIZE**

A

Match line AB

Center

B

Christmas Florals Tree Skirt

*As shown on page 142, skirt is
41 inches in diameter.*

MATERIALS
Transfer paper
Transfer pen
**1 yard of Zweigart hunter green
Punktchen Damask Dot fabric**
**1 yard of Zweigart cream Punktchen
Damask Dot fabric**
**1½ yards of 45-inch-wide ivory cotton
backing fabric**
**Cotton embroidery floss: Deep rose
(DMC 326) and medium pistachio
(DMC 367)**
**Kreinik metallic very fine No. 4 braid,
2 spools of No. 002J gold**
Size 22 chenille needle
Tracing paper
Hunter green sewing thread

INSTRUCTIONS
Trace embroidery
pattern, *page 156,* onto
transfer paper, following
manufacturer's instructions.
Transfer pattern eight times to
cream damask fabric, allowing
space all around for cutting out
embroidered pieces.

Embroider designs as follows:
using closed fly stitch, work petals
of center flower in red and large
leaves behind flower and along vine
in green; using stem stitch, work
vine and small lazy daisy leaves in
green; work lazy daisy flowers in
red; stitch all French knots using
gold very fine braid.

Trace partial
Pattern A, *above,*
onto tracing paper.
Match points A and B with
those on remainder of Pattern A,
opposite, and trace; cut out entire
Pattern A piece. Trace pattern B,
page 156, onto tracing paper and cut
out. Cut out embroidered flower

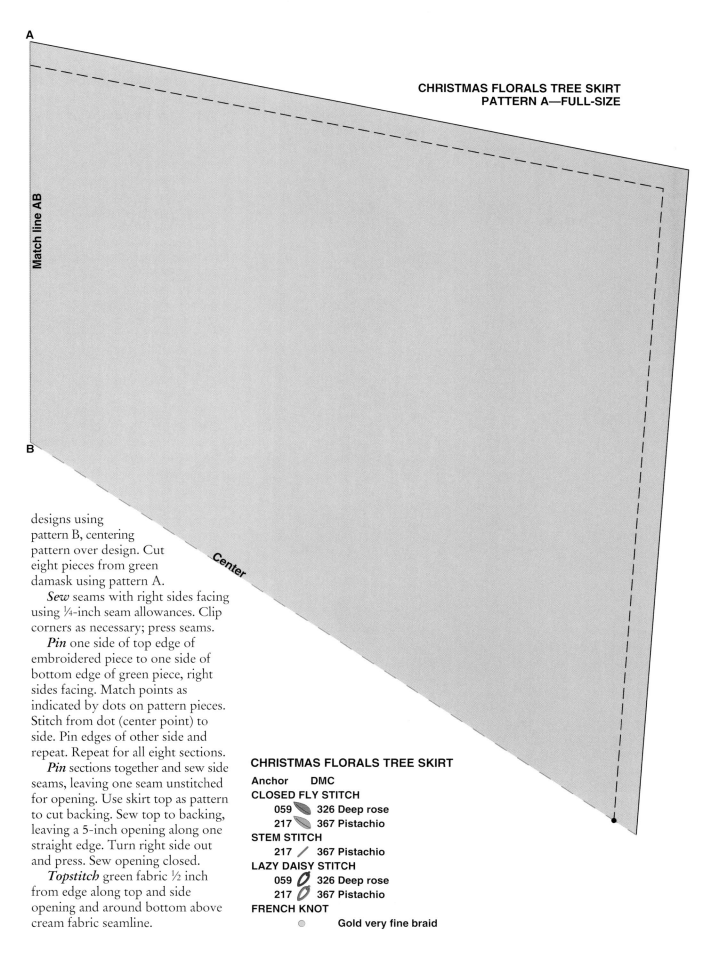

A

Match line AB

B

Center

designs using pattern B, centering pattern over design. Cut eight pieces from green damask using pattern A.

Sew seams with right sides facing using ¼-inch seam allowances. Clip corners as necessary; press seams.

Pin one side of top edge of embroidered piece to one side of bottom edge of green piece, right sides facing. Match points as indicated by dots on pattern pieces. Stitch from dot (center point) to side. Pin edges of other side and repeat. Repeat for all eight sections.

Pin sections together and sew side seams, leaving one seam unstitched for opening. Use skirt top as pattern to cut backing. Sew top to backing, leaving a 5-inch opening along one straight edge. Turn right side out and press. Sew opening closed.

Topstitch green fabric ½ inch from edge along top and side opening and around bottom above cream fabric seamline.

CHRISTMAS FLORALS TREE SKIRT

Anchor	DMC	
CLOSED FLY STITCH		
059		326 Deep rose
217		367 Pistachio
STEM STITCH		
217	/	367 Pistachio
LAZY DAISY STITCH		
059		326 Deep rose
217		367 Pistachio
FRENCH KNOT		
		Gold very fine braid

CHRISTMAS FLORALS TREE SKIRT
PATTERN B—FULL-SIZE

Center

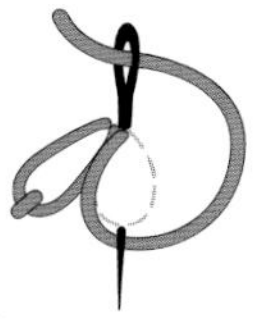

Lazy Daisy

French Knot

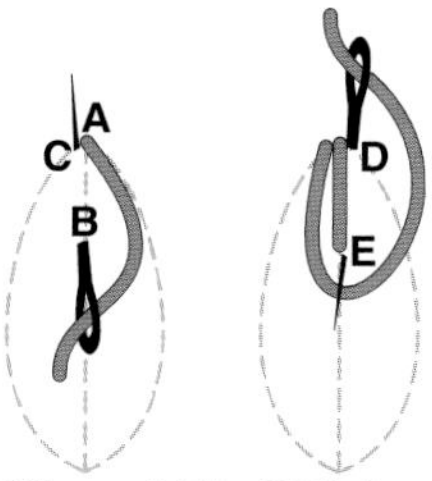

C A
B
D
E

Closed Fly Stitch

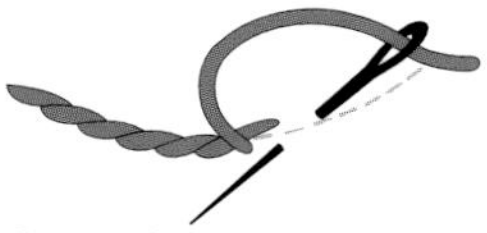

Stem Stitch

Beribboned Trim

As shown on page 143, ornament measures 4¼ inches in diameter.

MATERIALS
Five 6-inch-long pieces of ⅞- to 1½-inch-wide ribbon in bright Christmas colors
6x6-inch piece of lightweight fusible interfacing
Lightweight pressing cloth
Embroidery floss in desired colors
Gold metallic thread
Tapestry needle; beading needle
4¼-inch-diameter circle of clear plastic canvas
4¼-inch-diameter circle of fleece
4¼-inch-diameter circle of red or green felt
Assorted beads as desired for decoration
10 inches of ⅛-inch-diameter gold metallic cord
12 inches of ⅞-inch-wide gold ribbon
Three ½-inch-diameter colored jingle bells

INSTRUCTIONS
Arrange ribbons parallel to each other on the fusible side of the interfacing in a desired pattern, with the long edges touching. Cover with a pressing cloth and fuse the ribbons to the interfacing following the manufacturer's instructions.

Add desired decorative stitches to join long edges of ribbons, using floss or metallic thread. Use photograph, *page 143*, for ideas.

Lay plastic canvas on back of ribbon pattern and cut out circle, allowing ½ inch beyond plastic all around. Glue fleece to one side of plastic canvas. Center ribbon circle atop fleece; glue excess to back of plastic canvas. Hold ends of gold cord together and glue to back of ornament to make hanging loop. Glue felt to back, covering ends of cord.

Tie bow from gold ribbon; tack to ornament at base of hanging loop. Tack three bells to knot of bow. Sew beads to front as desired.

Whimsical Painted Chair

As shown on page 144.

MATERIALS

Adult wood chair
Sandpaper
Tack cloth
Acrylic wood primer
   (for painted base)
Wood stain
   (for stained base)
Acrylic paints in desired colors
Paintbrushes
Small natural cosmetic sponge
Drafting tape
Pencil
Wood beads or motifs, twine, 2 small
   screw eyes, and crafts glue
   (optional for hanging strand)
Clear acrylic spray varnish

INSTRUCTIONS

Sand the surfaces to prepare wood for painting; wipe with a tack cloth. For new wood to be painted, apply coat of primer; allow to dry. Apply desired base color to each section. Apply second coat if necessary and allow to dry. For wood to be stained, apply stain according to manufacturer's instructions; allow to dry.

Refer to photograph, *page 144,* and patterns, *right,* for design ideas. For spokes and legs, paint a variety of geometric or freehand designs, using several colors. Use tape as a mask and guide as necessary to create blocks of color. Add stripes of contrasting color; make polka dots using eraser end of pencil dipped in paint.

If desired, paint wood motifs and glue onto chair, using photograph for ideas. For a hanging strand as shown in photograph, thread painted beads and motifs onto twine. Knot each twine end onto screw eye which has been attached to chair.

After all paint is dry, spray entire chair with acrylic varnish.

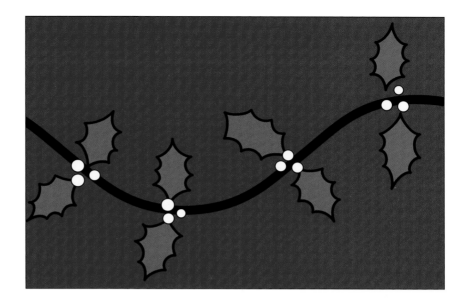

Christmas Rose Chair

As shown on page 144.

MATERIALS
Old or antique chair; sandpaper
Acrylic wood primer; soft rag
Acrylic paints; paintbrushes
Small natural cosmetic sponge
Stiff ½-inch flat paintbrush
Crafts knife; acrylic clear varnish
Gold Rub n buff highlighting medium

INSTRUCTIONS

Prepare surfaces if needed, by lightly sanding and priming the wood. Choose smooth surfaces to be painted deep red, such as front and back surfaces of legs, and front and back surfaces of vertical chair back pieces. These surfaces will be painted last.

When creating multi-colored relief sponge painting, it works best to reserve darkest colors for the deepest crevices, and layering the colors in order from darkest to lightest, using less paint for each consecutive layer, ending the last layer with the lightest color on the most raised surface.

To paint relief areas on chair, use a sponging technique. Use a palette of deep red, purple, pink, and yellow ochre, or an area like this rose. Use the very deep red for overall base color. Paint carved relief areas according to Step 1, *below*. To blend and highlight the colors, see Steps 2 and 3. Do not overwork. Allow the paint to dry.

To paint an area like the leaves, see Step 4.

For remaining surfaces, paint deep blue and sponge with thinned turquoise, using techniques as for relief areas; allow to dry. Next, paint the previously reserved areas deep red. Allow paint to dry thoroughly.

Follow Step 5 to spatter speckles on desired areas.

Seal chair with varnish. Using finger, very lightly apply a small amount of Gold Rub n buff to most raised areas. Rub off with a soft rag. Seal chair a second time.

Use deep and vibrant purples to paint the deep crevices. Apply these two colors quickly without allowing them to dry. The colors will somewhat blend together.

Before totally dry, but still tacky, use a clean water-dampened sponge and very lightly blend the purple and red together just enough to eliminate harsh brush strokes.

To highlight raised areas, use a sponge and thinned pink paint to gently dab on soft highlights. Repeat with a light ochre color. Do not overpaint.

Paint leaf areas with dark green, using dark blue for deep crevices; blend using a sponge. After dry, apply a light layer of turquoise and a light layer of lime green for highlights.

To splatter-paint surfaces, use a stiff, coarse paintbrush and deep red and metallic gold paints. Dip brush into one paint at a time. Use a crafts knife to scrape across the bristles.

Index

Sources

Candy Cane Scarf Set, page 8: Yarn—Spinrite Inc., P.O. Box 40, Listowel, Ontario N4W 3H3.

Dainty Welcome Towel, page 11: Fingertip towel—Charles Craft, Inc., P.O. Box 1049, Laurinburg, NC 28353; ribbon—Bucilla, 1 Oak Ridge Road, Hazleton, PA 18201-9764.

Cuddly Snowmen Sweater, page 14: Yarn—JCA, Inc, 35 Scales Lane, Townsend, MA 01469.

Country Christmas Paper Bags, pages 52–53: Felt—CPE, Inc. P.O. Box 649, Union, SC 29379; embroidery floss—The DMC Corporation; buttons—Streamline Buttons, 845 Stewart Avenue, Garden City, NY 11530-4878; beads—Gay Bowles Sales.

Warm Holidays Holly Afghan, page 117: Yarn—Coats & Clark, 30 Patewood Drive, Greenville, SC 29615.

Gift Wrap—Hallmark, call 800/HALLMARK to find the retailer nearest you.

Ribbon—C.M. Offray & Sons, Inc. Route 24, Box 601, Chester, NJ 07930-0601.

Needlework Projects

FABRICS
Charles Craft, P.O. Box 1049, Laurinburg, NC 28353, 800/277-0980; Wichelt Imports, Inc., R.R. 1, Stoddard, WI 54658; Zweigart, 2 Riverview Drive, Somerset, NJ 08873-1139, 908/271-1949.
THREADS
Anchor, Consumer Service Department, P.O. Box 27067, Greenville, SC 29616; DMC, Port Kearney Building 10, South Kearney, NJ 07032-0650; Kreinik Manufacturing, 800/537-2166.

Photographers

Hopkins Associates: Front cover and pages 14, 47, 50, 54, 62–65, 78, 80–83, 101, and 102.

Scott Little: Pages 6–8, 10–13, 15, 22, 23, 25, 27–33, 35, 37, 45, 46, 48, 49, 51–53, 61, 66–68, 77, 79, 89–92, 98, 99, 103–105, 108–110, 113–116, 119, 120, and 136–144.

Andy Lyons: Pages 9, 117, and 188.

Crochet Abbreviations

ch(s)—chain(s)
dc—double crochet
est—established
hdc—half double crochet
lp(s)—loop(s)
rem—remaining
rep—repeat
rnd(s)—round(s)
RS—right side
sc—single crochet
sk—skip
sl—slip
sp(s)—space(s)
st(s)—stitch(es)
tc—triple crochet
tr—treble crochet
tog—together
WS—wrong side
yo—yarn over

Knitting Abbreviations

beg—beginning
bet—between
cont—continue
dec—decrease
est—establish
inc—increase
k—knit
m—make
m1—make one
p—purl
pat—pattern
rem—remaining
rep—repeat
rnd(s)—rounds(s)
RS—right side
st st—stockinette stitch
st(s)—stitch(es)
tog—together
WS—wrong side